ANARCHY and APOCALYPSE

Mindy, God's peaceful anarchy to you from Ron!

ANARCHY and APOCALYPSE

Essays on Faith, Violence, and Theodicy

RONALD E. OSBORN

CASCADE *Books* • Eugene, Oregon

ANARCHY AND APOCALYPSE
Essays on Faith, Violence, and Theodicy

Copyright © 2010 Ronald E. Osborn. All rights reserved. Except for brief quotations in critical publications or reviews, no part of this book may be reproduced in any manner without prior written permission from the publisher. Write: Permissions, Wipf and Stock Publishers, 199 W. 8th Ave., Suite 3, Eugene, OR 97401.

Scripture quotations taken from the New American Standard Bible®, Copyright © 1960, 1962, 1963, 1968, 1971, 1972, 1973, 1975, 1977, 1995 by The Lockman Foundation. Used by permission." (www.Lockman.org)

Scripture taken from the New King James Version. Copyright © 1982 by Thomas Nelson, Inc. Used by permission. All rights reserved.

Cascade Books
An Imprint of Wipf and Stock Publishers
199 W. 8th Ave., Suite 3
Eugene, OR 97401

www.wipfandstock.com

ISBN 13: 978-1-60608-962-0

Cataloging-in-Publication data:

Osborn, Ronald E., 1975–.

    Anarchy and apocalypse : essays on faith, violence, and theodicy / Ronald E. Osborn.

        x + 164 p. ; 23 cm. —Includes bibliographical references and index.

        ISBN 13: 978-1-60608-962-0

        1. Christianity and politics. I. Title.

BR115 .P7 O83 2010

Manufactured in the U.S.A.

Contents

Preface vii

1. War, Fate, Freedom, Remnant 1
2. Bonhoeffer's Pacifism 15
3. The Christ of the Fifth Way: Recovering the Politics of Jesus 20
4. "May Fire Come Out from the Bramble": Notes on the Subversion of Political Authority in Israel's Royal History in the Hebrew Bible 44
5. Anarchy and Apocalypse: The Radical Social Ethics of an American Religion 51
6. The Death of a Peace Church 62
7. William Lloyd Garrison and the Problem of Constitutional Evil 68
8. Language in Defense of the Indefensible: Lessons from the Village of Ben Suc 91
9. Obama's Niebuhrian Moment 105
10. Geometries of Force in Homer's *Iliad*: Two Readings 116
11. The Trial of God: For Elie Wiesel 127

Bibliography 157

Index of Names 163

Preface

The essays and articles in this volume (with the exception of the final chapter) were written as responses to the terrorist attacks of September 11, 2001, and America's subsequent wars in Afghanistan and Iraq. These events, however, are only occasionally directly mentioned. My feeling from the start of the so-called "war on terror" was that what concerned people around the world—and religious persons in the United States in particular—most needed were tools of dissent based upon a longer view of history. I therefore tried in my writing to practice a kind of critical detachment from the grim revelations of the daily news cycle, not by affecting a spurious and pseudo-scientific "objectivity" but by searching primarily for analogies, memories, and allusions as a way of resisting the "principalities and powers" in Washington, London, Baghdad, and elsewhere. Hence, for example, as the bombs began to fall on Kabul in 2002 I decided to follow Simone Weil's lead at the start of World War II and begin by writing about Achilles, Hector, and the fall of Troy in Homer's *Iliad*. Whether or not this was the right approach I leave to my readers to decide. I hope, though, that by their nature the chapters that follow might provide helpful ways of thinking not only about the violence and suffering of the past eight years (continuing into the present), but more broadly about the violence and suffering of humanity at war with itself from the beginning of history as we know it.

I have arranged these essays according to themes and arguments rather than in a strictly chronological order. They vary greatly in style, length, and approach. All, though, focus on closely related questions. What are the underlying causes and consequences of violence? What kinds of moral and spiritual resources can persons of belief—and especially those of us in the Christian tradition—draw on in the face of dilemmas of injustice, inequality, and conflict? How should we respond

Preface

to the clamorous calls for obedience and allegiance assailing us from all directions? And what existential and moral crises must individuals of all faiths, or none, face up to in the age of Auschwitz, Hiroshima, My Lai, Rwanda, and Abu Ghraib?

If there is an underlying "project" in these essays it is an attempt to make clear the vibrant connections between nonviolent anarchist and Christian political thought as found in the Gospel narrative. I first began seriously thinking about the anarchist dimensions of the Christian *euangelion* while helping to coordinate emergency food and shelter relief for returning refugees with an international aid organization in Kosovo in the six months immediately after the end of the 1999 war. It was my first job out of college. Before leaving for the Balkans I had packed two books into my suitcase: *The Kingdom of God is Within You* by Leo Tolstoy and *The Chomsky Reader* by Noam Chomsky. Reading Tolstoy and Chomsky against a backdrop of destroyed Albanian villages set me thinking in earnest for the first time about the intractable moral and political problems generated not only by violence and war but by power itself, and to begin to reexamine nonviolence (I had already read a fair amount of Martin Luther King Jr. and Gandhi as an undergraduate) as a serious response to the many paradoxes, ironies, ambiguities, and temptations of power.

I later discovered thinkers like Jacques Ellul, John Yoder, Vernard Eller, William Cavanaugh, and Stanley Hauerwas, all of whom advocate some form of what might be described as Christian nonconformity with power if not Christian anarchism. But my interest in Chomsky in particular (who I have written about elsewhere[1]) grew out of my sense that, like the early pioneers of the Seventh-day Adventist church—the peculiar denomination in which I was raised and which continues to be animated by a distinctive apocalyptic imagination—he was engaged in a form of social and political critique that was not merely political but in fact *prophetic*. Hence the title of this collection, which reflects my own complex, highly personal, and ongoing attempt to work out the political implications of authentic (as opposed to apologetic or fundamentalist) apocalyptic and prophetic faith in a world of ferocious "beasts" ready to wage war with every imaginable tooth and claw—savage structural adjustment policies, "enhanced interrogation techniques," secret "renditions," "preci-

---

1. Osborn, "Noam Chomsky and the Realist Tradition," 351–70.

sion" bombing, massive military-industrial complexes supported by both major parties, and insurgency and counter-insurgency warfare.

There are many people to whom I owe gratitude for making this book possible. First and foremost, I want to thank my parents, Ken and Ivanette, my two sisters, Lorelie and Kim, and my grandparents, Robert and Evelyn Osborn. This book is dedicated to the memory of my grandfather, who was a conscientious objector and noncombatant medic during World War II. Sigve Tonstad generously read and commented on an early draft of this manuscript, for which I am grateful. I would also like to acknowledge some friends and mentors who have played particularly important roles in shaping and sharpening my ideas (not always by their agreement) over the course of my life: Roy Branson, Eric Guttschuss, Harry Leonard, Douglas Morgan, and Ottilie Stafford. Finally, I must thank the editors of the Adventist Peace Fellowship, *Spectrum Magazine*, *Humanitas*, the *Journal of Law and Religion*, *First Things,* and *Z Magazine,* which published earlier versions of some of these essays and have kindly permitted me to reprint them.

—2010

1 · *War, Fate, Freedom, Remnant*

I

Homer understood the logic of violence. In the *Iliad*, his epic retelling of the fall of Troy, every emotional, physical, and psychological dynamic of force is carefully and critically weighed. Every aspect of the human personality is submitted to the harsh rigors of close combat. Every ethical reserve is tested in the pitch of battle. Here, amid the crush of flesh and iron, ideals and abstractions are shattered in an ultimate realism. Lofty sentiments are unraveled by the elemental impulse for self-preservation. Moral pretensions and pieties are stripped bare by death feeding at the altar of war. The final vision of the poem, however, is not a celebration of this stark arena, or, as some have believed, of the soul of the warrior. It is, rather, an understanding that all who engage in violence are mutilated by it; that one cannot wield might without becoming its slave; that those who live by the sword shall die by the sword.

    We discover that this greatest of all war epics is in fact an antiwar epic not through any systematic exposition or declaration, but through a striking accumulation of detail. First, there is the fact that the entire conflict is waged for the sake of a symbol, Helen, rather than any objective purpose or moral necessity. Capricious gods—acting through their ciphers, the ruling elites—stir the masses of ordinary people into a positive desire to kill *and be killed*. The gods must continually prime these men for battle through high-sounding rhetoric, through oracles and omens and promises of glory and success. Yet the impulse to wage war defies any logic or reason external to the war itself. When left to their own intuitions, the common soldiers declare that their only desire is to abandon the campaign and set sail for home. At the gates of Troy we thus find ourselves in an ethical void in which violence serves as its own justifier. "You

Anarchy and Apocalypse

must fight on," the gods command, "for if you make peace you will offend the dead." It is slaughter, in other words, that necessitates more slaughter. Against the desire of the gods to maximize destruction is the suffering of the innocent, as when the aging King Priam gives the following grim account of what war can only mean for the vast majority of human beings:

> *Pity me too!—*
>
> *still in my senses, true, but a harrowed, broken man*
>
> *marked out by doom—past the threshold of age . . .*
>
> *and Father Zeus will waste me with a hideous fate,*
>
> *and after I've lived to look on so much horror!*
>
> *my sons laid low, my daughters dragged away*
>
> *and the treasure-chambers looted, helpless babies*
>
> *hurled to the earth in the red barbarity of war . . .*
>
> *my sons' wives hauled off by the Argives' bloody hands!*
>
> *And I, I last of all—the dogs before my doors*
>
> *Will eat me raw . . .* (22.68–78).[1]

The victims of war, Priam bears witness, are not the soldiers, whose deaths will be celebrated with songs and wreaths, but women, children, and the elderly. This, of course, comes as no new fact to anyone. But Priam's words are particularly penetrating and revelatory, for Priam is a Trojan, a foe of Homer's people. The foundational text in the Greek self-understanding subversively invites us to contemplate how violence bears on the weakest members of society and *even on the enemy*. It is as though the Hebrew Bible included descriptions of how YHWH's holy wars might have felt for a Philistine child.

Most subversive of all, however, is the way in which the *Iliad* plays havoc with the underlying assumption of what would later be known as the "just war" tradition, namely, the assumption of reason. All just war theories rest upon the idea that violence can somehow be contained within established rules of prudence and proportionality. But if violence serves as its own justifier, and if the suffering of the innocent is not enough

---

1. Fagles, trans., *The Iliad*.

War, Fate, Freedom, Remnant

to deter an initial act of aggression, there is no possible limit that can be placed on any war waged for "a just cause."

In Homer, this truth emerges through the unraveling of a treaty offering a modicum of ethical constraint within the conflict. Early in the poem the Greeks and Trojans make a pact allowing both sides to collect and burn their dead without hindrance or threat of attack. The agreement, while not affecting the actual prosecution of the war, seeks to place the struggle within the framework of social and religious convention. It aims to humanize and dignify the bloodshed through shared values of reason and restraint. Unfortunately, maintaining one's reason while drenched in human blood is a tenuous affair. As the war intensifies, the combatants kill with increasing savagery until at last they are seen gleefully mutilating dead corpses. "Go tell them from me,/ you Trojans, tell the loving father and mother/ of lofty Ilioneus to start the dirges in the halls!" cries Peneleos to the Trojans while holding up the fallen soldier's eyeball on the point of his spear (14.86–88).

When the Greek hero Patroclus is slain at the end of Book Sixteen the unstoppable drift toward total war, in which no rules or conventions apply, is finally realized. The two sides engage in a battle of unprecedented fury and destruction for the entirely irrational purpose of seizing Patroclus's dead body—the Trojans to further mutilate it and then feed it to wild dogs, the Greeks to prevent this humiliation at whatever cost. The idea that war might somehow be mediated by reasonable agreements and religious scruples, such as those governing the burial of the dead, has been reduced to a shambles by the internal dynamics of war and the logic of violence itself. [critique of just war]

Once this fact of war is understood, all of our long-cherished rationalizations for violence are quickly exposed as mere enervating chimeras. As goes the venerable Patroclus, so goes the tradition of just warfare. The failure of the tradition is not that it is abstractly or theoretically false, but that it ignores what actually happens when humans engage in violence. Philosopher and Christian mystic Simone Weil had a clearer view of the human animal. In "The *Iliad*, Poem of Might," her celebrated essay written at the onset of World War II, she saw that an excessive use of violence is almost never a political ideal, yet its temptation almost always proves irresistible—against all reason or moral restraint. "A moderate use of might, by which man may escape being caught in the machinery of its vicious cycle, would demand a more than human virtue, one no less rare

[weakened mythological horrible monster]

3

than a constant dignity in weakness," she wrote. As a consequence, "war wipes out every conception of a goal, even all thoughts concerning the goals of war."[2] Such a moral and spiritual void will, of course, be filled by politicians, militarists, and theologians with symbols and myths, but Weil understood that there is ultimately only one impulse strong enough to sustain wars among nations: the insatiable demand for power at any cost.

II

These insights are, I realize, difficult to grasp within the present national echo chamber of war enthusiasm, but they can be tested against the weight of history. Let us consider how prophetic Weil's thoughts about force proved in a war that most people agree was fought for a just cause if ever there was one.[3]

On September 11, 1944, Allied forces conducted a bombing raid on the city of Darmstadt, Germany. The incendiary bombs used in the attack came together in a conflagration so intense it created a firestorm nearly one mile high. At its center, the temperature was approximately 2000° F, and it sucked the oxygen out of the air with the force of a hurricane. People hiding in underground shelters died primarily from suffocation. People fleeing through the streets found that the surfaces of the roads had melted, creating a trap of molten asphalt that stuck to their feet and then hands as they tried to break free. They died screaming on their hands and knees, the fire turning them into so many human candles. Almost twelve thousand noncombatants were killed that night in Darmstadt alone. Yet Darmstadt was only one city among many in a relentless Allied campaign. Anne-Lies Schmidt described the aftermath of a similar attack on Hamburg, code named "Operation Gomorrah," more than one year before:

> Women and children were so charred as to be unrecognizable; those that had died through lack of oxygen were half charred and recognizable. Their brains tumbled from their burst temples and their insides from the soft parts under their ribs. How terribly

---

2. Weil, "The Iliad, Poem of Might," 168, 170.

3. The facts in this section have been adapted from Glover, *Humanity*, 69–116; McCullough, *Truman*, 391–96, 436–44, 453–60; and Merton, "Target Equals City," in *Passion For Peace: The Social Essays*, 28–36.

must these people have died. The smallest children lay like fried eels on the pavement. Even in death they showed signs of how they must have suffered—their hands and arms stretched out as if to protect themselves from the pitiless heat.[4]

That single raid on Hamburg killed approximately forty thousand civilians, including both of Schmidt's parents. In total, it is estimated that more than half a million German civilians were killed as a direct result of British and American bombing. What must be absolutely clear about these deaths is the well-documented but largely ignored fact that they were absolutely intentional. These were not unfortunate casualties in a campaign against German military targets: from as early as July, 1943, on, *they were the targets*. The saturation bombing of German cities did not include the burning of children as an unavoidable "double effect" of "Just War"; burning noncombatant men, women, and children was the precise strategy of Allied planners.

It did not begin this way. At the start of the Battle of Britain in 1939, leaders on both sides declared that they would not target civilian populations. It was understood that bombing military factories and installations would result in unavoidable civilian casualties. But the policy of minimizing deaths among noncombatants was widely supported by both politicians and the public on religious and ethical grounds. This course continued until August 24, 1940, when Luftwaffe bombs, intended for an oil storage depot, fell on London's East End. Winston Churchill, overruling the Royal Air Force, ordered a bombing raid on Berlin the next day. Germany responded by unleashing the blitz over London. Still, for some months the RAF insisted that the ban against killing civilians was still in effect. There was a lingering sense of moral compunction among the Allied forces that the dynamics of violence had not yet fully eroded. This would change.

First, because it was too risky to bomb by day, the Allies decided that bombing should be done only at night. This, however, made precision bombing impossible and proved militarily unsuccessful since targets were often missed. Realizing that their efforts to strike only military targets by cover of darkness were not working, the RAF therefore shifted to a policy of "area bombing." The destruction of whole neighborhoods was now permitted, providing there was a single military target within a given

4. Glover, *Humanity*, 78.

Anarchy and Apocalypse

neighborhood. But by 1942, with the war dragging on and casualties mounting, the Allies decided that even this was not enough. Abandoning any pretense of ethical standards, they adopted a more "realistic" policy once and for all: indiscriminate "obliteration bombing" of entire cities. The explanation given for the new phase in the Allied campaign was twofold: first, it would ensure absolute success against military targets; more importantly and explicitly, it would "break enemy morale." Chivalric distinctions between civilians and combatants were no longer practicable. The morality of "total war" was tautologically justified by the necessity of "victory at any cost."

So began the routine bombardment of noncombatants. Yet soon Churchill was calling for still greater innovations in violence. "I should be prepared to do anything that might hit the Germans in a murderous place," he wrote to his Chiefs of Staff in July, 1944:

> I may certainly have to ask you to support me in using poison gas. We could drench the cities of the Ruhr and many other cities in Germany in such a way that most of the population would require constant medical attention . . . It is absurd to consider morality on this topic when everybody used it in the last war without a word of complaint from the moralists or the Church. On the other hand, in the last war the bombing of open cities was regarded as forbidden. Now everybody does it as a matter of course. It is simply a question of fashion changing, as she does between long and short skirts for women.[5]

In the end, the Allies were unable to devise a feasible plan for chemical war, but not for lack of will or trying. They were hampered, in Churchill's words, by "that particular set of psalm-singing uniformed defeatists," and by logistical considerations within the military. "I cannot make headway against the parsons and the warriors at the same time," he lamented.[6] The aerial campaign against civilian populations meanwhile proceeded without dissent. What feeble resistance there was to the policy of "total war" was kept to a minimum through pressure tactics and facile slogans. This will end the war sooner. This will save lives. We must take retribution. We must punish the aggressor. There were, it should be noted, a surprisingly high number of RAF pilots and crews who objected to the terroristic annihilation of defenseless noncombatants now required of

---

5. Gilbert, *Churchill*, 782–83.
6. Ibid., 783.

6

them. But the military took severe disciplinary action against these individuals, court-martialing and imprisoning them to prevent their strange ideas from spreading through the ranks. The official reason given for their punishment was "LMF"—lack of moral fiber.

In the Pacific arena, however, moral fiber was in abundant supply. On the night of March 9, 1945, the United States set the entire city of Tokyo ablaze with napalm bombs. The heat was so intense it boiled the water in the canals. More than 100,000 civilians died in the attack. Bomber crews in the last waves could smell the burning flesh. The same was done to more than fifty other Japanese cities, leading to a befuddling dilemma for Allied strategists: by May and June there were few "untouched" cities left for the ultimate demonstration of Allied "resolve." At last a list of cities, including the religious center of Kyoto, was compiled and submitted to the American High Command. None were proposed for primarily military reasons. What was critical in each case was that the target included a massive unspoiled population that could be annihilated without warning in a single moment. Civilian morale and psychological considerations—terrorism to be precise—dictated where the atomic bombs would fall.

The strategy was a spectacular "success." More than 350,000 civilians were killed in Hiroshima and Nagasaki in a litany of unspeakable horror, some instantly in the inferno that consumed the cities at the speed of two miles a second; some more slowly, their skin hanging from their bodies like rags; some vomiting and convulsing from radiation sickness days later; some bleeding out of the retina, the mouth, the rectum, and respiratory passages from decay of internal organs; others later still from cancer and unknown diseases. For years afterward thousands of children conceived in the two cities were born with chromosomal and genetic disorders—a multigenerational reminder of American power and so added insurance policy against recalcitrant Japanese nationalism.

In five short years between 1940 and 1945 the cycle of violence had come full circle. The Allies began the war vowing that they would not use the techniques of their enemies, but in the end the logic of violence proved irresistible. Their cause was just. Their motives were pure. But the initial cause of war proved immaterial to the way in which the war was finally waged. Once violence was accepted as a means to an end, violence became its own end. Traditional morality was discarded as so much intellectual and spiritual deadweight. "If [the Japanese] do not now accept our terms they may expect a rain of ruin from the air, the like of

Anarchy and Apocalypse

which has never been seen on this earth," said President Harry S. Truman in his radio broadcast to the nation.[7] The nation applauded. A poll in *Fortune* magazine suggested that the only regret of nearly a quarter of the American public was that more atomic bombs had not been used. Truman, for his part, insisted that after ordering the bombings he went to bed and slept soundly.

The point is not that Allied soldiers lacked moral principles, goodwill, or noble intentions. It is that war has its own will and its own intentions: it refuses to be contained or controlled by mere humanity. Whatever vestiges of decency and restraint America and England possessed at the start of the war gave way to more pragmatic calculations as the war progressed. Sentimental images of American GIs dispensing chocolate bars to German and Japanese children prevents us from seeing the staggering slaughter inflicted by the Allies, with absolute calculation, on hundreds of thousands of civilians.

All of the arguments dredged up from medieval scholastic theology to vindicate violence for "a just cause"—and particularly World War II—therefore miss the mark. The ethical principles set forth for defending stone castles, if ever valid, were rendered obsolete by the advent of modern war. As Thomas Merton wrote in his essay "Target Equals City":

> There is one winner, only one winner in war. The winner is war itself. Not truth, not justice, not liberty, not morality. These are the vanquished. War wins, reducing them to complete submission. He makes truth serve violence and falsehood. He causes justice to declare not what is just but what is expedient as well as cruel. He reduces the liberty of the victorious side to a servitude equal to that of the tyranny which they attacked, in defense of liberty. Though moralists may intend and endeavor to lay down rules for war, in the end war lays down rules for them ... War has the power to transmute evil into good and good into evil. Do not fear that he will not exercise this power. Now more than ever he is omnipotent. He is the great force, the evil mystery, the demonic mover of our century, with his globe of sun-fire, and his pillars of cloud. Worship him.[8]

---

7. McCullough, *Truman*, 455.

8. Merton, *Passion for Peace*, 28.

III

But is there any alternative? Do we have any choice other than violence? When Hitler and Hirohito unleashed their war machines on the world, what else could be done? If not retaliation in kind, what then? If not retributive justice, how peace? Before attempting to give a positive answer, we must return to the world of *Iliad*. We must see why the question suggests the same fatalism that permeated ancient Greek thought.

For the Greeks, over and against the will of the gods was the inexorable reality of Fate or *Moira*. Fate, armed with necessity (*ananke*), joins with the Furies (*Erinyes*) to defy human craft and intelligence. Even Zeus is unable to overrule what Fate commands. In Plato's *Timaeus*, for example, it is the task of the Creator or Demiurge to mold blind, inert matter to the divine will. But matter, *ananke*, is resistant to any meaning or purpose, so the creation is never wholly good or complete; there always remains in the universe a residual amount of "brute fact" or necessity that even the gods cannot rationalize or control. Ultimately, then, the highest provenance is not the divine will but the law of Fate. It is impossible to predict what Fate will command. It is impossible to argue with what Fate decrees. "Fate is immutable, impersonal, unseeing, and strikes like a thunderbolt. Future is like past: determined."[9] In the *Iliad*, the war is not spurred on primarily by human choices, but by the edicts of Fate meted out by Zeus. Achilles, Zeus declares to the goddess Hera, will not fight until after Hector kills Patroclus "in the narrow place of necessity . . . This is the way it is fated to be." In the meantime, the Furies must ensure that the war does not come to a premature end; so "Terror drove them, and Fear, and Hate whose wrath is relentless . . . the screaming and the shouts of triumph rose up together/ of men killing and men killed, and the ground ran blood" (4.440–451).[10] Homer sees how abhorrent war is, but he is unable to posit any escape from it; the cycle of violence is senseless but unavoidable.

Several centuries later, this idea of the simultaneous futility and inescapability of bloodshed would form the heart of Greek tragedy. Aeschylus's *Oresteia* trilogy is archetypal: Agamemnon sacrifices his daughter Iphigeneia to propitiate the goddess Artemis. His wife Clytaemestra must then murder him to avenge the death of her daughter.

---

9. Heschel, *The Prophets: Volume II*, 19.
10. Lattimore, trans., *The Iliad of Homer*.

Anarchy and Apocalypse

But Orestes, prompted by Apollo, must now kill Clytaemestra to avenge Agamemnon. The cycle is only ended by the arbitrary intervention of the goddess Athene, who appeases the Furies by giving them a permanent home beneath the city of Athens.

The contemporary question of whether there is any alternative to violence (and the assumption that the answer is negative) is best seen in this mythological context. For when we examine the statements made by politicians and military planners in World War II, what is most striking is not the fact that they made dubious ethical choices, but that often in the deepest sense they did not make choices at all. "Truman made no decision because there was no decision to be made," recalled George Elsey, one of his military advisors involved with the Manhattan Project. "He could no more have stopped it then a train moving down a track . . . It's well and good to come along later and say the bomb was a horrible thing. The whole goddamn war was a horrible thing."[11] So, we discover, from the *Iliad* to Dresden and Nagasaki nothing has changed. Roosevelt, Churchill, and Stalin met at Malta. Fate, necessity, and the Furies decided the war.

This is why violence, at its most basic root, is the ultimate form of passivity. It is based upon the assumption and the fear that when Fate decrees slaughter, humans have no choice but to obey. The "realist" is a conscientious objector to nonviolent action because ultimately he does not believe we are truly free. To think "pragmatically" about when it is acceptable for innocent humans to be destroyed is to think mechanistically about what it means to be human. "War always encourages a patriotism that means not love of country but unquestioning obedience to power," writes Kentucky farmer-philosopher Wendell Berry. "In the face of conflict, the peaceable person may find several solutions, the violent person only one."[12] Christian complicity in the atrocities of our century thus reveals how deeply the church has absorbed the pagan malaise of determinism. By rejecting nonviolence as a binding principle, Christians have cauterized their consciences and absolved themselves of the freedom to make authentic moral choices. Can the passivity of the German population in World War II be separated from Martin Luther's claim that Christians are duty bound to wield the sword for the sake of political and social order? Can the compliance of the Catholic chaplain who ad-

---

11. McCullough, *Truman*, 442.

12. Berry, "Peaceableness Toward Enemies," in *Sex, Economy, Freedom and Community*, 77, 87.

ministered mass to the Catholic crew that dropped the atomic bomb on Nagasaki (destroying three orders of nuns in the process) be separated from Augustine's Just War teaching? "[S]hould you see that there is a lack of hangmen," Luther wrote in 1523, "and find that you are qualified, you should offer your services."[13] The Protestant Church has been offering its services ever since. The Catholic Church had a head start beginning with Constantine in the fourth century.

IV

So again, the question: is there any alternative to violence and the fatalism it implies? The New Testament witness says there is. This witness, however, does not take pragmatic reason as its highest value and starting point. Rather, it declares that reason itself is defined by the life and teaching of a single person. One may, of course, reject this person's teaching of peaceableness toward enemies. What one cannot legitimately do is deny what this teaching *is*. The evidence is absolute and unequivocal; all special pleading for violence must studiously refrain from sustained exegetical analysis:[14]

> You have heard that it was said, "An eye for an eye, and a tooth for a tooth." But I say to you, do not resist an evil person; but whoever slaps you on your right cheek, turn the other to him also . . . You have heard that it was said, "You shall love your neighbor and hate your enemy." But I say to you, love your enemies and pray for those who persecute you, so that you may be sons of your Father who is in heaven. (Matt 5:38–39, 43–45a)[15]

The Sermon on the Mount, from which these words are taken, is presented in Matthew's Gospel in a programmatic fashion as the new Torah, a new charter for the community of believers. Just as Moses delivered the tablets of stone from Sinai, Jesus gathers his disciples on the mountain to disclose a new covenant with Israel. The new covenant begins with the Beatitudes, a counterintuitive and politically charged overturning of the world's values and moral reasoning. God's blessings, Jesus declares, are

---

13. Luther, *Martin Luther*, 374.

14. See Hayes, *Moral Vision of the New Testament*, 317–43; and Yoder, *Politics of Jesus*.

15. All biblical citations are from the New American Standard Bible unless otherwise noted.

upon the downtrodden, the oppressed, the meek, the peacemakers. All of the accouterments of power and prestige on display in Greco-Roman society mean nothing. Education, wealth, and noble pedigree are illusory anchors. Lord Caesar and Lord Mammon are out. Reality, in God's eyes, is ordered with a paradoxical premium upon weakness and undeserved suffering.

To embody God's truth in a blinded world, Jesus calls for the formation of a countercultural community, "a *polis* on a hill" (Matt 5:14). In the *polis* of Jesus, reconciliation will overcome hostility, marriage vows will be kept with lifelong fidelity, language will be honest and direct, all hatred and violence will be renounced. The emphasis throughout is not upon individual piety as a means to salvation, but upon personal and social ethics leading to restored community in the present reality. Jesus sees his teaching as the deepest fulfillment and revelation of the Law and the prophets. He does not seek to negate the Torah but actually *intensifies* the Torah's demands. The Law prohibits murder; Jesus prohibits even anger. The law prohibits adultery; Jesus prohibits even lust. When it comes to the matter of violence, however, Jesus does not simply radicalize the Torah: he decisively alters and in fact overturns it.

The *lex talionis*—an eye for an eye, a tooth for a tooth—is spelled out in several passages in the Hebrew Bible, but particularly in Deut 19:15–21. If in a criminal trial a witness gives a false testimony, the Law declares, that person must be severely punished in order to preserve the social order. "Thus you shall not show pity: life for life, eye for eye, tooth for tooth, hand for hand, foot for foot" (19:21). Political stability is the goal and fear is the mechanism by which it will be achieved. Jesus shatters this strict geometry with a simple injunction: "Do not resist an evil person." This does not imply passive capitulation to force, but physical nonretaliation as a dynamic spiritual weapon, particularly in the political realm. The command only makes sense in the context of the prophetic community or *polis* Jesus has announced he is building. By exemplifying the peaceableness and conciliatory spirit of the Beatitudes, the believer confounds and shames the aggressor, creating an opportunity for the violent person to be reconciled with God. By absorbing undeserved suffering and not retaliating in kind, the disciple also destroys the evil inherent in the logic of force. Instead of an endless cycle of violence and recrimination, there is *shalom*, there is peace.

The assumption among believers that violence is an acceptable tactic and tool, and the willingness of the Christian community to play chaplain to our nation's military complex, therefore discloses a crisis of mistaken identity. When Christians declare that "we" must wage war for the sake of this or that political goal, when they point to what "they" did to "us" and argue about what "our" response should be, they mistakenly identify the calling of believers with the objectives of the nation-state. But the *polis* of Jesus is not merely one kind of allegiance contained within others, wheels within wheels. It is a radically different allegiance based upon goals and principles that the state may at times not tolerate or comprehend. In the final analysis, because nonviolence may result in martyrdom as it did for Jesus, it only makes sense to those who see all war in "cosmic perspective," who know that there is genuine freedom because there is also Advent hope.

The freedom of the prophetic community is not freedom from "this-worldliness." It is not liberty for the sake of personal security or individual purity. It is not motivated by narrow perfectionism or pious idealism. Rather, those who are truly free are conscious that they must live as faithful witnesses amid all of the ambiguities and anxieties of society, speaking truth to power in a fallen world and acting in ways that might actually make a difference. This means challenging the unquestioning raptures of a war-worshiping culture. This means proclaiming the principles of the Sabbath Jubilee as God's judgment upon social and economic systems that oppress and exploit. This means fighting for peace using the weapons of peace rather than the weapons of death and fear.

The hope of nonviolent resistance to evil is not unrealistic, as history has proved. The accomplishments of Gandhi and Martin Luther King are well known, but there have been many others. During World War II, the French Huguenot village of Le Chambon Sur Lignon saved thousands of Jewish children through nonviolent noncooperation with Gestapo and Vichy authorities. The entire nation of Denmark likewise engaged in nonviolent resistance to the Nazis. When told that Jewish refugees must wear stars, the Danes declared that they would all wear stars; they mounted strikes and protests; they refused to repair German ships in their shipyards; they ferried Jews to Sweden out of harm's way; they hid Jews in their homes. Again, thousands of lives were saved. Nazi officials were thoroughly unnerved, bewildered, and deflated by these actions. Many were converted. Eichmann was repeatedly forced to send specialists to

Anarchy and Apocalypse

Denmark to try to sort out the problem since his men on the ground could "no longer be trusted."[16] These movements, however, were rooted in communities that took their Christianity seriously and were prepared to count the cost. Let us cease praying for the success of our technology and weaponry long enough to ponder: are Christians still ready to count the cost?

—2002

---

16. See Arendt, *Eichmann in Jerusalem*, 171–75; and Merton, "Danish Non-Violent Resistance to Hitler," in *Passion for Peace*, 150–53.

2 · *Bonhoeffer's Pacifism*

In times of war, Dietrich Bonhoeffer is sometimes cited as an example of authentic Christian resistance to tyranny through the tactics of force. In a July 11, 2003, *Washington Post* article, provocatively entitled "Bonhoeffer: Thou Shalt Kill," Philip Kennicot writes that any serious debate about violence and nonviolence must deal with the question: What about Hitler? Bonhoeffer, he suggests, offers a compelling example of a conscientious Christian concerned with radical discipleship who nevertheless saw that violence was morally justified in the face of Nazi evil. Political philosopher Jean Bethke Elshtain has also invoked Bonhoeffer's name as a rebuke to Christian pacifists and as a summons for believers to embrace the necessity of force in America's "war against terrorism." The United States and its military arsenal, she writes, offer the only assurance of "international civic peace."[1] "For Christians living in historic time and before the end of time, the pervasiveness of conflict must be faced," Elshtain continues. "One may aspire to perfection, but living perfectly is not possible . . . For St. Augustine, for Martin Luther, and for the anti-Nazi martyr Dietrich Bonhoeffer, the harsh demands of necessity as well as the command of love require that one may have to commit oneself to the use of force under certain limited conditions, and with certain intentions."[2]

In sharp contrast with Elshtain and others who have sought to appropriate Bonhoeffer for the "realism" of the just war tradition, James William McClendon in his *Systematic Theology* (1986) sees Bonhoeffer's final political actions as exhibiting a tragic loss of nerve and loss of faith that can in no way be reconciled with the demands of the Gospel. The German pastor's participation in the *Abwehr* plot against Hitler, McClendon writes,

---

1. Elshtain, *Just War Against Terror*, 6–7.
2. Ibid., 101.

15

Anarchy and Apocalypse

"was not only inconsistent with Bonhoeffer's long-formed Christian convictions but was ineffectual as well."[3] For McClendon, Bonhoeffer's theological ethics were so heavily reliant upon the practices of the Christian community *as a community* that when the German church "crumbled under government pressure, he no longer had any resource for *Christian* resistance." Thus, "he turned to the time-honored practices and skills of his family, and to the 'practice' (if it was that) of the *Putsch*, for which neither he nor his family and friends had sufficient skills of any sort."[4] Far from offering an exemplary justification for forceful opposition to evil, then, Bonhoeffer's role in the conspiracy to assassinate Hitler, in McClendon's view, must be "understood as a remarkable, sinful failure in his life."[5]

It may be, though, that the challenge of Bonhoeffer's life for believers wrestling with questions of violence and war is more challenging than either Elshtain's or McClendon's readings allow. Bonhoeffer would certainly not have accepted the distinction of "just warrior" Elshtain wishes to bestow on him. He, of all Germany's wartime thinkers, believed that neither the church nor society could survive through compromises and utilitarian calculations, as must invariably be made by those who embrace acts of violence in the name of preserving social order. Bonhoeffer's theology, Stanley Hauerwas has shown, continues to offer critical resources for persons committed to the ethics of Christian nonviolence.[6] At the same time, I want to explore the possibility that Bonhoeffer's final political *actions*—distressing and problematic for pacifists as they may be—might have been consistent at some level with his earlier theological writings and also stand as part of Bonhoeffer's witness for peace.

Bonhoeffer expressed his commitment to Christian pacifism from the moment the National Socialists seized control in Germany. When asked by a student in 1934 what he would do if there was war, Bonhoeffer, breaking sharply with Luther's doctrine of obedience to the state, replied: "I will pray that God will give me the strength not to take up arms."[7] Yet Bonhoeffer knew that war was likely and so that same year corresponded with Gandhi, arranging to visit him in India to study his methods, which

---

3. McClendon, *Ethics*, 209.
4. Ibid., 210.
5. Ibid., 211.
6. See Hauerwas, "Dietrich Bonhoeffer," 136–49.
7. As cited in Wind, *Dietrich Bonhoeff*, 93.

Bonhoeffer's Pacifism

he hoped to use against the Nazi government. The trip never occurred, but between 1935 and 1936 Bonhoeffer joined with several friends in Germany to form the House of the Brethren, a social movement based upon the teachings of the Sermon on the Mount. In 1937, as the noose of Nazi tyranny tightened, Bonhoeffer's *Cost of Discipleship* was published in which he charted a radical social ethic for believers, including nonviolence as a Christian imperative.

Bonhoeffer's hope of Christian nonviolent resistance to fascism was not unrealistic, as history has proved. The French Huguenot village of Le Chambon Sur Lignon, whose story is told in Philip Hallie's *Lest Innocent Blood Be Shed*, saved thousands of Jewish children through nonviolent noncooperation with Gestapo and Vichy authorities. The entire nation of Denmark, Hannah Arendth reported in *Eichmann in Jerusalem*, likewise engaged in effective nonviolent resistance to the Nazis. Yet these pacifist responses to Hitler's assault were rooted in Christian communities where the church could still be counted on for support and moral guidance. After Hitler's lightening-swift victory over France in 1940, and the jubilant or passive response of his fellow German Christians, Bonhoeffer realized that the ground had fallen out from under believers in Germany. It remained his conviction that the church must be a radical witness against violence. But with the church scattered and in disarray, the situation bore in on him as a personal ethical crisis: was it better for him to participate in the resistance, or to maintain his ethical rigorism in the face of Hitler's atrocities?

There was no acceptable answer to the question in Bonhoeffer's mind. He did not doubt that violence and coercion are tools denied believers in the New Testament. But, he understood, to not allow himself to become guilty of violence might be the greatest guilt of all. "The great masquerade of evil has played havoc with all our ethical concepts," he wrote several months before his arrest in 1943. Germans faced a situation in which "every available alternative seemed equally intolerable, repugnant, and futile."[8] These words are from Bonhoeffer's essay, "After Ten Years," a declaration of spiritual and ethical convictions in the form of a letter to his close friends, which some theologians consider his finest work. In this brief meditation, Bonhoeffer rejects the idea that "civil courage" requires prudential or self-interested calculations of the sort secular

---

8. Bonhoeffer, *Letters and Papers from Prison*, 16.

"realism" demands. "Who stands fast?" he asks. "Only the man whose final standard is not his reason, his principles, his conscience, his freedom, or his virtue, but who is ready to sacrifice all this when he is called to obedient and responsible action in faith and in exclusive allegiance to God—the responsible man, who tries to make his whole life an answer to the question and call of God."[9]

What exactly did Bonhoeffer mean by "exclusive allegiance" to "the question and call of God"? The answer is not at all clear, but Bonhoeffer's statement may have reflected the influence of the great Swiss theologian, Karl Barth. According to Barth, the responsibility of the Christian in times of war is never to justify but always "to manifest a distinctive horror of war and aloofness from it."[10] Pacifism, Barth taught, is the rule of the Christian life. The Kingdom of God, of its very nature, stands over and against all human pretensions to power and control by force. And yet, Barth maintained, no word of God can be made absolute by humans in a way that limits the freedom of God to speak a new word in "an exceptional case." Hence, the Christian must be a pacifist yet at the same time cannot be an "absolute" pacifist since this would amount to a denial of God's freedom to be God.

Barth's theology of the *Grenzfall*, the exceptional case, tempts the kind of casuistry that politicians, generals and theologians have resorted to throughout history to justify acts of violence by the state. But neither secular realism nor natural law categories of "just war" were what Barth had in mind when he spoke of God's freedom to speak a new word. Rather, Richard Hays writes in *The Moral Vision of the New Testament*, his account of the moral life demands "a constant reliance on prayer and listening for the guidance of God, believing that God can and does address individuals specifically with particular instructions." Hence, "we read Scripture thoroughly with the intent of obeying exactly what is commanded there, while always listening prayerfully for the unlikely revelation that in a particular case we may be commanded to do something contrary to the rule given by Scripture."[11]

Was Bonhoeffer's participation in the Officer's Plot final proof, then, of the failure of Christian pacifism in the face of radical evil? Or was he in

---

9. Ibid., 19.

10. As cited in Hays, *Moral Vision of the New Testament*, 233.

11. Ibid., 233.

fact a living example of the Barthian "exceptional case"? Bonhoeffer's own words in "After Ten Years" suggest that his subjective experience during the plot against Hitler was very much that of an exceptional summons. His spiritual and moral breakthrough came not as a reasoned move in the direction of universal ethics, but as a sudden awareness of God's Real Presence and the divine call to an excruciating action in his particular circumstance. Examined closely, "After Ten Years" is therefore the very antithesis of every rationalization for violence, not least those offered by Bonhoeffer's fellow clergymen in support of Hitler. Bonhoeffer was, by his own account, engaged not in an act of "just warfare" but in an existential "venture of faith." Significantly, he did not act with any expectation of success (a central requirement in just war thinking as developed by the Catholic Church). Nor did he see his actions as presenting a model for others to imitate. Rather, like Abraham binding Isaac to the altar, he saw his complicity in the plot against Hitler as the peculiar and terrible cross he and he alone was called to bear.

In the end, it was a cross in every sense. On April 9, 1945, Bonhoeffer was executed by the SS at Flossenbürg concentration camp for treason against the state. Yet Bonhoeffer's witness lives on as pacifists and non-pacifists alike continue to wrestle with his challenging insistence on obedience to God's call amid all of the tensions and ambiguities of history.

—2004

3 · *The Christ of the Fifth Way*

Recovering the Politics of Jesus

Many Christians throughout history have tried to separate the Gospel as a matter of spiritual truth from the realm of earthly politics, yet there is little in what Christ said and did that does not have profound political implications for his followers. The more we understand about the world of first-century Palestine and the Roman empire into which Jesus was born, the more clear it becomes, in fact, that the New Testament was written as a subversive alternative political grammar for God's people. Jesus tells his disciples they should be like an independent Greek city-state, like a *polis* on a hill (Matt 5:14). Paul's chosen word for the church, *ecclesia*, did not originally mean a building of worship but a deliberative assembly, a political council-meeting concerned with the matters of community.[1] "The difference between church and state or between a faithful and an unfaithful church," John Howard Yoder writes, "is not that one is political and the other not, but that they are political in different ways."[2] Protestants since Martin Luther have often ignored or suppressed the politics of Jesus, declaring that salvation is a matter of being "born again" through a purely individual response "by faith" in Christ's death. But we must recover the politics of Jesus as central to our understanding of the Gospel lest we fool ourselves into thinking we can be saved by faith in a Jesus whose *life* we have never encountered.

---

1. Meeks, *Origins of Christian Morality*, 45.
2. Yoder, *Body Politics*, ix.

The Christ of the Fifth Way

Life in the Occupied Territories

The world of first-century Palestine, against which the Gospel narratives are set and the meaning of Jesus's life must finally be reckoned, was divided into two broad categories of people: the rich few and the poor many. The rich minority included several high-priestly clans, who controlled the Temple in Jerusalem and exercised a monopoly over the economy of worship and sacrifice; the Herodians, who ruled Palestine at Rome's behest and owned more than half of the land; and a small number of other land-owning Jewish aristocrats. These wealthy elites were bitterly resented by the rest of the population, which was comprised of some poor craftsmen, rural priests, farmers, fishermen, and others who managed a modest but tenuous existence, and a much larger number of day-laborers, subsistence farmers, and socially marginalized groups, who even in the best of times lived on the very edge of survival. It was into this broad class of poor people that Jesus, according to the Gospel of Luke, was born. At his dedication in Jerusalem, his parents could not afford to buy a lamb, the prescribed offering, and so sacrificed the poor people's offering of two birds instead (Luke 2:24).

The poor majority—the peasant masses described as the "people of the land" in rabbinic literature—were heavily taxed by both secular and religious authorities. They were subjected to frequent exploitation and debt-bondage by state bureaucrats and wealthy creditors. They confronted a situation of increasing crime, family breakdown, environmental stress and untreatable diseases.[3] And they bore the brunt of Rome's degrading and brutal military occupation, which began in 63 BCE with Pompey desecrating the Holy of Holies and continued through 135 CE when Hadrian finally decimated Jerusalem once-and-for-all, forcing the surviving Jews into slavery or exile from which they would not regain control of Palestine until the twentieth century.[4]

The Romans did not normally send their legions to physically occupy conquered lands, ruling instead through efficient laws, economic pressure, and military bases strategically positioned as "deterrent forces" around the periphery of the empire.[5] But in the always volatile region of Palestine, Roman legions were a constant presence in the role of foreign

---

3. Horsley and Silberman, *Message and the Kingdom*, 3.
4. Wright, *New Testament and the People of God*, 159, 165–66.
5. Horsley, *Jesus and Empire*, 22.

Anarchy and Apocalypse

"peacekeepers." Throughout Jesus's life, Jews faced routine harassment, violence and humiliation by these Roman soldiers, including forced conscription as baggage porters, a problem Jesus directly addresses in the Sermon on the Mount (Matt 5:41).

Especially galling for pious Jews was the way the pagan occupiers stamped the images and iconography of their imperial cult upon the Jewish landscape. The Law of Moses forbids visual representations not only of God, but of all living creatures.[6] But Jewish religious sensibilities were continually being affronted by the presence of blasphemous imperial standards, votive shields, statues and other forms of artwork proclaiming Caesar's victories and divine title: DIVI FILIUS—"son of god." Roman imperial imagery across the Mediterranean world was often pornographically violent in nature, with conquered nations being depicted as violated women at the feet of the divine Caesar himself.[7] The ultimate goal of imperial symbolism, however, was not simply to humiliate Rome's defeated enemies but to integrate them as subjects of Roman patronage in a "civilized" world order. Jews had little choice, for example, but to use Roman coinage stamped with Caesar's portrait and images of Roman gods and goddesses. Since possessing or even handling these coins was deeply problematic for strict commandment-keepers, devout Jews were daily forced to compromise their beliefs and collude with the pagan occupiers in order to survive.[8] They were forced to barter their faith in order to participate in the marketplace of Rome's new global economy.

Unsurprisingly, feelings of righteous anger, humiliation, and hatred were always boiling just beneath the surface. Under these circumstances, seemingly trivial but symbolically potent acts, such as the placement of Roman standards near the Temple in Jerusalem, could spark furious (and in the eyes of the Romans, fanatical) riots. These violent demonstrations sometimes led to pragmatic concessions from the authorities, whose official policy was one of tolerance for the Jewish religion. More often they were crushed by tactics of shock and awe—spectacles of overwhelming military might, of which public crucifixion was but one conspicuous example. Immediately after Herod the Great's death—during Jesus's infancy

6. See Heschel, "Symbolism and Jewish Faith," in *Moral Grandeur and Spiritual Audacity*, 80–99.

7. Crossan and Reed, *In Search of Paul*, 267–69.

8. Cullman, *Jesus and the Revolutionaries*, 45–48; Wright, *Jesus and the Victory of God*, 506.

The Christ of the Fifth Way

in either Egypt or Nazareth—Judean peasants rose up in a campaign of violent resistance against the Romans and their Jewish puppet regime. The result was over 2,000 insurgents being crucified outside Jerusalem.[9]

The idea that Jews in Jesus's day were primarily concerned with matters of dogmatic theology, or that first-century Judaism stood for salvation by "works" as opposed to "faith," N. T. Wright concludes, must therefore be rejected. "[T]he pressing needs of most Jews of the period had to do with liberation—from oppression, from debt, from Rome."[10] The burning question on people's minds was: How will God act, *in history*, to save the Chosen People from their enemies, both within and without? One's theological answer to this question revealed one's political ideology, while one's politics conversely revealed one's theology. In first-century Palestine, the two were always and inseparably entwined. Between Herod the Great's death in 4 BCE and the first destruction of Jerusalem in 70 CE, Israel was convulsed by repeated religious revolts, violent messianic movements, political assassinations, insurgency and counter-insurgency warfare. In short, if we think about present-day Palestine, and the kinds of political paths that might tempt a poor but religiously devout Palestinian young man in the West Bank or Gaza Strip, we will not be far from understanding the historical reality that confronted Jesus, a young Jewish carpenter living in the occupied territories approximately two thousand years ago.

Collusion and Compromise: The Way of the Herodians

In his novel *The Last Temptation of Christ*, Nikos Kazantzakis imagines a Jesus whose greatest temptation is to get married, to settle down, to raise a family and experience a comfortable and conventional life into old age. There is little in the New Testament, though, to suggest that Jesus was ever strongly tempted by such a prosaic vision. What the Gospels do suggest is that Jesus was repeatedly tempted to embrace the agendas and tactics of several competing theological-political movements, each claiming to know how best to realize God's kingdom on earth. The political significance of Jesus's kingdom announcement emerges in sharp relief

---

9. Stambaugh and Balch, *New Testament in Its Social Environment*, 24–26.
10. Wright, *New Testament and the People of God*, 168–69.

Anarchy and Apocalypse

when we consider four rival kingdom programs or paths he might have chosen instead.

First, Jesus might have followed the path of pragmatism or "realism" represented by the Herodians and Sadducees. These political and religious authorities (successors to the dynastic line of Babylonian Jews known as the Hasmoneans) had no legitimate claim to rule other than having colluded with the foreign invaders. They administered Judea on Rome's behalf and, like the Vichy government in occupied France, were viewed as traitors and collaborators by the rest of the population. Thomas Cahill describes them as a "gang of priest-pretenders" whose piety "was not so much suspect as nonexistent."[11] Yoder, however, offers a more nuanced reading. It is superficial, he argues, to dismiss the Herodians and Sadducees merely as scheming, morally bankrupt pawns of the Caesars. These were in fact intelligent planners, men who understood balances of power and the necessity of following a "responsible strategy."[12] Their moral assumption was that people needed to face up to "reality": when you cannot achieve your ideals, you must learn to work within the realm of the possible, to form unpleasant alliances if necessary and to accept "dirty hands." According to Josephus, the Sadducees believed in "free will," which Wright interprets not as an abstract metaphysical claim but as the belief that God helps those who help themselves.[13]

In many ways, the Herodian approach to building God's kingdom "worked." Because of their willingness to collude with Rome, they managed to maintain the Temple in Jerusalem and to secure official recognition of the Jewish faith. It is the seeming effectiveness of the Herodian option, the way of "conscientious cooperation," that makes it such a tempting path, in all ages, for individuals who want to act responsibly to change the world. Nevertheless, in the final analysis, Herodian "realism" was not realistic enough to save Israel from the impending cataclysm. Realism, as a secular political doctrine, asserts that humans are capable of calculating and balancing means and ends, tactics and goals, in proportional and effective ways. *Biblical realism,* however, declares that the pretensions of the hard-headed "realists" are in fact hopelessly naïve and idealistic; humans are unable to control or contain the outcomes of their

---

11. Cahill, *Desire of the Everlasting Hills*, 40.
12. Yoder, "Original Revolution," in *For the Nations*, 169.
13. Wright, *New Testament and the People of God*, 211.

choices, particularly when violence is involved.[14] Further, by working for incremental change *within* the Roman system of coercion and violence, the Herodians lost their ability to challenge the system itself. They were easily co-opted as *conservatives*, as apologists for empire and the status quo.

But Jesus was not a defender of the status quo. Nor was Jesus co-opted by empire. In the story of his confrontation with Satan in the wilderness at the start of his public ministry—which, whether read literally or allegorically, clearly reveals the early Christian view of political power—Jesus rejects the path of political compromise, the way of collusion with the kingdoms and governments of this world. In the Lukan version of the story, Satan shows Christ "all the kingdoms of the world in a moment of time" and tells him that "all this domain and its glory" "has been handed over to me, and I give it to whomever I wish" (Luke 4:5–6). Jesus, amazingly, does not dispute Satan's claim. The subversive implication, Jacques Ellul suggests, is that the devil is speaking the truth.[15] All human systems of power and control, without exception, are seen as falling under the domain of the enemy. But Jesus, quoting from the book of Deuteronomy (4:8), declares that humans were made to serve God alone. The only escape from the imperialist-nationalist trap is for believers to pledge a radically different allegiance.

Sons of Light: The Way of the Essenes

The fact that disciples are called to a radically different allegiance than that of state, party, "civilization," or empire has tempted many believers down another perilous path, a path that was also fully open to Jesus in first-century Palestine. At the opposite end of the political spectrum from Herodian pragmatism lies the path of quietism or sectarian withdrawal represented by the group known as the Essenes, whose stringent way of life came to light in 1947 when a Bedouin shepherd boy stumbled upon a library of papyrus scrolls in the caves of Qumran near the Dead Sea south of Jericho.

This sect of ultra-orthodox Jews sought to live totally apart from the entanglements of the world by forming isolated, self-supporting commu-

---

14. Carter, *Politics of the Cross*, 31, 85.
15. Ellul, *Anarchy and Christianity*, 57–58.

nities in the Judean desert. They developed an apocalyptic and remnant theology according to which they alone were the chosen "sons of light" called to resist the "sons of darkness" in fulfillment of Isa 40:3: "Clear the way for the Lord in the wilderness. Make smooth in the desert a highway for our God." The Essenes saw themselves as the true heirs of historic Judaism and thus strove to maintain the Sabbath, and the dietary and purity laws of Moses in the face of what they perceived as rampant backsliding. God had providentially called their movement into existence, they believed, as the first phase in the restoration of Israel. They eagerly waited for the day when God's two Messiahs (both a priestly Messiah and a Davidic King) would arrive to conquer Rome and punish all those lax Jews who had failed to keep the commandments properly.[16]

The Essenes thus held no love for the Roman occupiers, or for the politically and theologically compromised Herodians. Yet precisely because of the strong future orientation of their eschatology, the Essenes during Jesus's lifetime did not participate in armed revolts or political agitation against the authorities; Herod was sufficiently pleased with their brand of sectarian withdrawal to grant them a special exemption from the oath of loyalty to himself.[17] What shrewd politician, after all, would seriously mind a community like that of the Essenes? Instead of revolutionary action in the name of divine justice, here was a group of people marked by their punctilious Bible study in remote caves, their strange but harmless calculations from prophecy of when the Messiahs would appear and by the fact that they held common meals together. The Essenes' withdrawal from social and political concerns in the name of religious purity was, ironically, its own brand of collusion with the political establishment. Silence and withdrawal, we find, are themselves highly political acts, often with devastating consequences for others.[18]

While the Essenes excluded all non-members—all those "sons of darkness"—from their table fellowship, Jesus, however, provoked scandal

---

16. Cohn, *Cosmos, Chaos and the World to Come*, 188–93.

17. Wright, *New Testament and the People of God*, 206. Concern for ritual purity would, however, ultimately lead the Essenes to political intransigence and violent conflict with Rome. In 68 C. E., the Romans destroyed the Qumran settlements and liquidated their inhabitants. See Cohn, *Cosmos, Chaos and the World to Come*, 191.

18. See Heschel, "Reasons for My Involvement in the Peace Movement," in *Moral Grandeur and Spiritual Audacity*, 224–26; and King, "A Time to Break Silence," in *A Testament of Hope*, 231–32.

The Christ of the Fifth Way

by freely associating with sinners and hosting meals for tax collectors. Jesus's path was not the path of retreat into the desert in the name of maintaining personal or communal purity—a choice that would have allowed the principalities and powers in Jerusalem to continue on with business as usual. Instead, Yoder writes, Jesus "set out quite openly and consciously for the city and the conflict which was sure to encounter him there."[19] Central to Jesus's kingdom announcement—which must be seen in the tradition of the Hebrew prophets who condemned the injustices and violence of Israel's rulers, and who suffered ridicule and martyrdom as a result—was the message that God does not desire ritual piety or scrupulous law-keeping but a people committed to acts of justice and mercy (Matt 9:13).

The Ghetto or the Sword: The Ways of the Pharisees

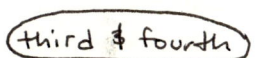

Somewhere between the sheer pragmatism of the Herodians and the sectarian withdrawal of the Essenes we find the ways of the Pharisees. The broad agenda of the Pharisees was close in many ways to that of the Essenes. They too despised the religious-political compromisers, as much if not more than their pagan overlords, and they struggled to preserve Jewish identity in the face of imperial pressure. But while the Essenes proclaimed, in effect, "Just wait: God will bring about Israel's liberation in his own time," the Pharisees, like the Herodians, were prepared to take a more active and urban role as political agents of God's will.[20] When God finally did intervene to restore Israel, the Pharisees maintained, he would restore the nation as a whole, not merely a sectarian elite sequestered in the Judean hinterlands.

The Pharisees divided into two major schools of political thought. The first, following the teachings of the Rabbi Hillel, sought to avoid direct confrontation with Rome, emphasizing instead the importance of Torah study, religious purity and political prudence. These Pharisees sought to strengthen Jewish piety with a view to resisting Roman oppression, but only when absolute essentials of the faith, "religious liberty issues," were at stake. In the eyes of these guardians of "proper" religion, Jesus was a threat who needed to be eliminated not only because he played fast and

---

19. Yoder, "Original Revolution," 173.
20. Wright, *New Testament and the People of God*, 200–201.

Anarchy and Apocalypse

loose with Sabbath, purity and dietary laws (Mark 2:23–28; 7:1–19), but because his band had all the hallmarks of a radical political movement that would soon attract the heavy hand of Rome (Luke 13:31). Better, they decided in council with the Sadducees (normally their bitter foes) on the Sanhedrin, Israel's highest political body, that "one man die for the people, and that the whole nation not perish" (John 11:50).

Other Pharisees, however, did not shy so quickly from the prospect of a "clash of civilizations" between Israel and Rome. These individuals, drawing their inspiration from the teachings of the Rabbi Shammai, urged immediate and violent revolt against Rome in the pattern of Judas Maccabaeus, who had led a seemingly miraculous guerrilla uprising against the Syrian megalomaniac Antiochus Epiphanes in 164 BCE (the event still celebrated by Jews during the festival of Hannakuh). Where the Hillelites represented the way of respectable or proper Judaism—the way of Mishnah and ghetto—these latter Shammaite Pharisees stood for revolutionary zeal, the way of the sword. The Apostle Paul, before his conversion, appears to have been one such Shammaite, fully prepared to use violence to rid Israel of apostates and traitors.[21]

The revolutionary zeal of the Shammaites was especially appealing to marginalized Jews living outside of the major centers of power—rural people in "underdeveloped regions" like Galilee, who fueled the economic dynamism of the empire by providing cheap labor and raw goods for export.[22] Fully half of Jesus's disciples may have had strong zealot leanings, if not outright zealot commitments.[23] Beyond what may be inferred from

---

21. The counter argument is that, according to the book of Acts (22:3), Paul studied at the feet of Gamaliel, who was a disciple of Hillel. Yet Paul says he persecuted the church "beyond measure" and went "beyond many of my contemporaries among my countrymen, being more extremely zealous for my ancestral traditions" (Gal 1:13–14). These statements of "extreme zeal" suggest that Paul was drawn to the more violent side of fundamentalist Judaism associated with Shammai. "[F]or the first-century Jew," Wright points out, "'zeal' was something you did with a knife." Wright, *What St. Paul Really Said*, 27.

22. Horsley and Silberman, *Message and the Kingdom*, 25–26.

23. Horsley and Hanson argue that it is misleading to speak about "Zealots" during Jesus's lifetime since the Zealots proper only emerged as a self-identified group in the mid to late 60s CE. But this point, Wright shows, should not obscure the historical reality of "zealots" (lower case "z") in Jesus's day, or the widespread tradition of violent zealotry that began several centuries before Jesus and extended throughout the first-century. See Horsley and Hanson, *Bandits, Prophets, and Messiahs*, 247–48; and Wright, *New Testament and the People of God*, 179–81.

The Christ of the Fifth Way

the disciples' social backgrounds, there are clues scattered throughout the Gospels. James and John urge Jesus to rain destruction on a group of offending Samaritans (Luke 9:51–56). Peter, along with James and John, is prepared to violently resist Jesus's arrest in Gethsemane (Luke 22:49). One or more of these three is armed with a sword and wounds a slave of the high priest (Matt 26:51–52). Simon is directly identified as a zealot (Mark 3:18). Some scholars have gone so far as to suggest that Judas Iscariot's name contains a veiled allusion to the *Sicarii*, a band of urban intellectuals turned terrorist-assassins with dynastic links to Judas the Galilean, the failed messianic leader executed for sedition against Rome in 6 CE, whose sons were also crucified for their politics in the 40s.[24]

The fact that Jesus attracted individuals such as these, who harbored violent insurrectionist dreams, and who probably hoped that alignment with Jesus would help to realize them, as well as the fact that Jesus's opponents could plausibly accuse him before Pilate of sedition against Rome, the legal charge on which he was finally crucified, points to the revolutionary nature of Jesus's character and kingdom announcement. But while Jesus is repeatedly tempted in the Gospels to take up the sword—to launch a campaign of "just war" that will vindicate the Jewish faith once and for all—he steadfastly refuses the path of coercive power, the way of violence to establish God's kingdom on earth (Matt 5:9, 38–48; 26:51–53; Luke 6:27; 22:50–53).[25] Precisely because he is so deeply sympathetic with the insurgents, the religious freedom fighters, he is also in many ways most critically opposed to them.

But what path *did* Jesus take to build God's kingdom? If not the way of the Herodians (calculation and compromise), the way of the Essenes (retreat into the desert), the way of the Hillelite Pharisees (Torah study and respectable religion), or the way of the zealots (violent revolution or "just war"), what other possible way? We have already begun to formulate a picture of Jesus's politics by way of negation and contrast as: (1) demanding a radically different allegiance than that of nation, state, party or empire; (2) engaging rather than retreating from concerns of social justice; and (3) refusing the path of political violence and coercive power. But

---

24. If this intriguing speculation is correct, the allusion would have to be a highly anachronistic one since the *Sicarii* only launched their terrorist campaign in the 50s CE, before the Gospels were written but well after Jesus's life and death. See Horsley and Hanson, *Bandits, Prophets, and Messiahs*, 200–207.

25. Stassen and Gushee, *Kingdom Ethics*, 20, 41, 152–55; Yoder, *Politics of Jesus*, 46.

what made the Way of Jesus—the word used by the earliest Christians to describe their faith—a compelling message of good news for people living in a situation of crushing poverty and foreign military occupation?

The Politics of the Kingdom

Centuries before Jesus's birth, Jewish apocalyptic writers struggled to understand the theological meaning of Israel's exile in Babylon. They concluded, with paradoxical audacity, that pagan oppression was the result not of YHWH's weakness but of his justice and strength: Israel was being punished by the Creator God for its failure to keep the covenant.[26] Things would grow progressively worse, Jewish eschatology predicted, until a final, decisive moment when God would at last send a warrior-prince to restore his Chosen People to their rightful place among the nations. Jewish apocalyptic literature used cosmic and fantastic images to describe this future event, but Jewish hopes were firmly rooted in the realm of concrete, earthly politics. When God's kingdom arrived, it would be plain for all to see by three material facts: 1) the Davidic monarchy would be restored in Jerusalem with unparalleled justice and prosperity; 2) the Temple would be rebuilt with unsurpassed splendor; and 3) the downtrodden Jews would emerge a triumphant superpower with their pagan enemies humiliated and defeated beneath them.

Jesus shared many of the basic assumptions of this traditional Jewish eschatology. He declared that oppression would increase before finally being overcome by God's saving activity (Mark 13:7–13). He urged his disciples to be steadfast and courageous in the face of evil (Matt 10:16–42). And he taught them to pray not for a "spiritual" kingdom somewhere in the sky but for God's kingdom to come "on earth as it is in heaven" (6:10). When Jesus talked about the kingdom, though, he did not talk about it in the future tense. Israel was still suffering under foreign oppression, economic injustice and religious corruption. But when Jesus talked about the kingdom he talked about it like it was going on then and there. He talked about it like it had already arrived. Even more shocking, the Gospel writers record, Jesus talked and acted like the kingdom was happening *in* him and *through* him. "But if I cast out demons by the finger of God," Jesus said, "then the kingdom of God has come upon you" (Luke 11:20).

26. Cohn, *Cosmos, Chaos and the World to Come*, 143, 73, 193.

The Christ of the Fifth Way

Jesus's kingdom announcement implied that conventional Jewish eschatology, with its vision of two successive historical ages, was either deeply flawed or had been gravely misread. Hebrew apocalyptic literature had depicted the coming of YHWH's kingdom as a dramatic, earth-shattering event that would radically divide the old aeon from the new. But Jesus declared, against all of the seeming evidence, that the kingdom of God was an already present, in-breaking reality, manifest in his own life and program of miraculous healings, and best grasped through metaphors of secrecy, simplicity and subversion. The kingdom, Jesus said, is not like a conquering army but like a mustard seed that inexorably consumes the garden (Luke 13:19). It is like the yeast or leaven that invisibly causes bread to rise (Matt 13:38). It is like a pearl of great price hidden in a field so that only the passionate seeker will find it (Matt 13:46).

In first-century Palestine, anyone talking about "the kingdom" was, by this fact alone, treading on perilous political ground. Caesar Augustus had already staked out Rome's exclusive claim to kingdom vocabulary, and the cult of the emperor brooked no rivals. Caesar was, according to one public inscription, "the beginning of all things"; "god manifest"; the "savior" of the world who "has fulfilled all the hopes of earlier times"; the one whose birthday "has been for the whole world the beginning of the good news (*euangelion*)."[27] We should not be surprised, then, that Jesus encoded his kingdom politics in parables, metaphors, riddles, and cryptic sayings that did not explicitly defy Roman rule. But for those who had ears to hear, mustard seeds and pearls of great price were the rhetoric of a revolution. Jesus—the true Savior of the world—was calling for his followers to embody YHWH's actual kingdom of compassion and justice *as over and against Lord Caesar's blasphemous parody*. He was telling them to incarnate God's reign in history by building a new kind of community—a countercultural "*polis* on a hill" (Matt 5:14)—that would stand in nonviolent but subversive opposition to all those forces responsible for grinding down the poor, the weak, the ritually unclean and sinners of every kind.

The fact that Jesus calls for his followers to incarnate or embody God's kingdom as a social reality in the present does not contradict but defines and animates Christian hope in the Parousia as a future event in space-time. According to John Dominic Crossan, Jesus proclaimed a *sapiential* as opposed to *apocalyptic* eschatology. *Sapientia* is the Latin

---

27. Horsley, *Jesus and Empire*, 24–25.

word for "wisdom," and according to Crossan Jesus offered human beings "the wisdom to discern how, here and now in this world, one can so live that God's power, rule, and dominion are evidently present . . . *rather than* a hope of life for the future" (my emphasis).[28] But the Jesus of the New Testament—the only Jesus we know[29]—offers his disciples both a Way of living that manifests God's kingdom in the midst of the present reality *and* a hope for the future that invests this Way with its power and meaning. It is precisely because of their confidence in the Parousia that believers are free to live out the dangerous and demanding politics of the Gospel. Conversely, it is only the social witness of believers that manifests Jesus's life and lordship over history to a watching world. Absent such a witness, Martin Luther King Jr. saw, there can be no authentic Advent hope. "Any religion that professes to be concerned about the souls of men and is not concerned about the slums that damn them, the economic conditions that strangle them and the social conditions that cripple them is a spiritually moribund religion awaiting burial."[30]

"The Favorable Year of the Lord": Economic Justice

In the Gospel of Luke, Jesus's first action at the start of his public ministry is to enter the synagogue in his hometown of Nazareth and read from the prophet Isaiah: "The Spirit of the Lord is upon me, because he anointed me to preach the Gospel to the poor . . . to set free those who are oppressed, to proclaim the favorable year of the Lord" (Luke 4:18–19). Only real debt-cancellation would have come as real good news for real poor people, Ched Meyers points out.[31] When Jesus claims the "favorable year of the Lord" as central to his vocation he is therefore not assuming a "spiritual"

---

28. Crossan, *Who Killed Jesus?*, 46–47.

29. See Luke Timothy Johnson's critique of Crossan and others who purport to reconstruct the "real" Jesus behind the New Testament texts by applying highly subjective techniques of literary analysis based upon a priori philosophical assumptions, which they then misleading describe as the "discoveries" of "historical" scholarship. It will be clear from what I have already written that I believe it is necessary to read the Gospels in historical context and alongside non-canonical works (for which Crossan's work is often helpful). However, Johnson points out, we should not distort "the very concept of history by insisting on discovering history where it cannot be found." See Johnson, *Real Jesus*, 101.

30. King, "Pilgrimage to Nonviolence," in *A Testament of Hope*, 38.

31. Meyers, "Jesus' New Economy of Grace," 36–39.

The Christ of the Fifth Way

as opposed to a *political* messianic role. He is, rather, directly alluding to a powerful vision of social justice contained in the Law of Moses that had been systematically suppressed and evaded by Israel's ruling elites for hundred of years, an economic ethic that would have come as welcome news indeed to the impoverished and exploited peasant masses of Galilee and Judea.

The "favorable year of the Lord" in Luke-Isaiah, Andre Trocmé and John Yoder show, is the Sabbath year or year of Jubilee commanded by God in the Hebrew Bible (particularly in Leviticus 25 and Deuteronomy 15).[32] Every seventh year, according to the Covenant, Israel was to enact a program of radical debt forgiveness, and in the fiftieth year land redistribution to benefit the poor. Among God's people, there was to be a systematic leveling of wealth on a regular basis and dismantling of what we would today describe as *oppressive financial and banking institutions designed to maximize profits for creditors.* Jesus does not attempt to instate these Jubilee commandments in a rigid or programmatic way, but he does reclaim the basic principles, metaphors and imagery of the Sabbath Jubilee for his followers.[33] He has more to say in the Gospels about issues of wealth and poverty than any other topic—and his message remains as challenging for those of us who live in affluent countries today as it was for the wealthy Herodians and Sadducees in first-century Palestine.

Against the assumptions of laissez-faire capitalism—which posits a world of unlimited human needs, individualism, and competitive rivalry for scarce resources—Jesus declares that we are stewards rather than owners of property, that God's creation is abundant and our earthly needs limited, and that God's liberation of Israel from slavery is normative for how we should treat the poor among us. His warnings against capital accumulation and "Lord Mammon" are unrelentingly severe (Matt 6:16–24; Mark 10:23–25). He tells his followers to live lives of dangerous generosity, giving and expecting nothing in return (Luke 6:30). He tells them to forgive each other's debts (Matt 6:12), to not worry about their own material needs but to live out a lifestyle of trust and simplicity (6:25–34; 10:9–10). And he instructs them to actively pursue justice (23:23). Material care for the poor, the oppressed and the hungry, Jesus

---

32. Trocmé, *Jesus and the Nonviolent Revolution*, 11–38; Yoder, *Politics of Jesus*, 60–75.

33. Wright, *Jesus and the Victory of God*, 295.

33

Anarchy and Apocalypse

declares, is the primary mark of discipleship—and the only question at the final judgment (25:31–40).

Jesus's radical economic teachings were epitomized among his early followers in the practice of "breaking bread," which was not originally merely a rite of sacral liturgy or mystical symbolism but an actual meal embodying Jesus's ethic of sharing in ordinary day-to-day existence.[34] When the Holy Spirit is poured out at Pentecost in the book of Acts, the practical result is that believers voluntarily redistribute their property. "And all those who believed were together, and had all things in common; and they began selling their property and possessions and were sharing them with all, as anyone might have need . . . breaking bread from house to house, they were taking their meals together with gladness and sincerity of heart" (Acts 2:44–46). The Apostle Paul also emphasizes the socio-political nature of the Lord's meal, delivering a blistering rebuke to those upper-class Corinthians who excluded poor believers from their table fellowship and sated their own stomachs while other members of the community went hungry (1 Cor 11:18–22).

"You Are All One in Christ": Equality in the Body of Believers

We can begin to see, then, why Jesus's message had such an electrifying effect on the impoverished and socially marginalized peasants of first-century Palestine who flocked to hear him speak—and why he so frightened and angered those guardians of public "order" for whom divisions of wealth and class were a useful rather than an oppressive reality. But Jesus challenged not only structures of economic injustice and inequality in first-century Palestine. He challenged patterns of social inequality, hierarchy and domination of every kind. In his treatment of women, of children, of Romans, of the ritually unclean and sinners of every stripe, Jesus repeatedly and provocatively overturned deeply ingrained cultural and religious assumptions about who was "first" and "last," "above" and "below" in the eyes of God.

There is no place in God's in-breaking kingdom, it turns out, for "great men" or "rulers" who "lord it over" others through the exercise of political or religious authority. Such, Jesus tells his disciples, is the way of the "Gentiles," i.e., the pagan unbelievers and Romans occupiers. But

---

34. Yoder, *Body Politics*, 20.

The Christ of the Fifth Way

among his followers, Jesus declares, "whoever wishes to become great among you shall be your servant and whoever wishes to be first among you shall be your slave" (Matt 20:25–28; Mark 10:43). Jesus goes so far as to command his followers to avoid using honorific titles of any kind, including the title of "leader." The only title Jesus permits is an address of familial equality and solidarity: "brother" (Matt 23:6–10). In the *polis* of Jesus, the New Testament suggests, there simply are no individuals in positions of status or hierarchical control.

Instead of offices, the earliest Christian communities appear to have been ordered along quasi-familial lines and according to the idea of spiritual *gifts*, including gifts of teaching, preaching, and stewardship. Spiritual gifts are charismatic, functional, provisional, and divinely rather than humanly bestowed. They are not restricted to special classes, genders, or tribes; for "There is neither Jew nor Greek, there is neither slave nor free man, there is neither male nor female; for you are all one in Christ" (Gal 3:28).[35] The most prominent functionaries in the early church, the "elders" or *presbyteroi* who helped to preside over the households where the early Christians gathered, were to lead by humble *example* rather than by "lording it over" the younger believers (1 Pet 5:1–3). The title of "priest" or *hiereus* (the root from which the English word "hierarchy" derives) is not applied to any particular Christian in the Gospels or Pauline corpus (although in Acts 6:7 we read that "a great many of the priests" in Jerusalem became "obedient to the faith," and in Rom 15:16 Paul describes himself by way of metaphor as a *minister* who works "as a priest" presenting God with "my offering of the Gentiles").[36] Jesus is the only person who is described (in the book of Hebrews) as a priest for the church; but he is the final priest who makes all priesthood obsolete—not merely the performance of ritual sacrifice, but the office, pomp and circumstance of priestly authority and hierarchy itself. Instead of deferring to any caste of religious hierarchs, followers of the Way are thus now summoned to

---

35. For women in particular, Christian community offered much greater equality with men, both by elevating their social and political status relative to men and by limiting the generally accepted freedoms of men in Greco-Roman society (e.g., to engage in premarital and extramarital affairs and to force their wives to abort unwanted children). As a result, during the first several centuries of Christian growth women were much more likely than men to convert to Christianity. See Stark, *Rise of Christianity*, 95–129.

36. See Wills, *What Jesus Meant*, 68–71. Confusingly, and despite much of his own evidence, Wills elsewhere asserts that Jesus's kingdom announcement was not political but wholly "spiritual."

collectively *be* a "royal priesthood," a "chosen race" or "holy nation" built not upon offices of any kind but upon transferred allegiance to God's in-breaking "kingdom" (1 Pet 2:9; Rev 1:6).

"Do Not Resist an Evil Person": Nonviolent Enemy Love

It was the fatal error of many Latin American liberation theologians to conclude from Jesus's concern for economic justice and his summons to radical, non-hierarchical community formation that the Way of Jesus may be harmonized with the way of violent revolt against oppressive social, economic and political structures. But Jesus of Nazareth, unlike Judas the Galilean, taught his disciples to turn the other cheek, to put away their swords and to love their enemies as themselves. Perhaps the most important hallmark of the politics of Jesus lies in his teaching and example of nonviolent enemy love.

Jesus's ethic of nonviolence finds its fullest statement in the Sermon on the Mount, which is presented in Matthew's Gospel in a programmatic fashion as the new Torah, a definitive moral charter to guide the community of believers.[37] Jesus does not seek to negate or overturn the Law of Moses with his own novel teaching but to reclaim the deepest meaning of the Law by intensifying and internalizing its demands. The Law forbids murder, Jesus forbids even anger. The Law forbids adultery, Jesus forbids even lust. When it comes to the matter of violence, though, Jesus may actually overturn the teaching of the Hebrew Bible. It is possible to read the Law of Moses as seeking to limit retribution, which would make Jesus's absolute prohibition on revenge also an intensification of the earlier commandment. It is equally possible to read Jesus's words as a decisive alteration, on this point and this point alone, of an earlier Jewish understanding.

> You have heard that it was said, "An eye for an eye, and a tooth for a tooth." But I say to you, do not resist an evil person; but whoever slaps you on your right cheek, turn the other to him also . . . You have heard that it was said, "You shall love your neighbor and hate your enemy." But I say to you, love your enemies and pray for those who persecute you, so that you may be sons of your Father who is in heaven. (Matt 5:38–45)

---

37. Hays, *Moral Vision of the New Testament*, 321.

The Christ of the Fifth Way

As I wrote in chapter 1 of this volume: "The *lex talionis*—an eye for an eye, a tooth for a tooth—is spelled out in several passages in the Hebrew Bible but particularly in Deuteronomy 19. If in a criminal trial a witness gives a false testimony, the Law declares, that person must be severely punished in order to preserve the social order. 'Thus you shall not show pity: life for life, eye for eye, tooth for tooth, hand for hand, foot for foot' (19:21). Political stability is the goal and fear is the mechanism by which it will be achieved. Jesus shatters this strict geometry, however, with a startling injunction: 'Do not resist an evil person.' This does not imply passive capitulation to violent people but physical non-retaliation as a dynamic and creative force in human relationships. By exemplifying the courage and forgiveness of the Beatitudes, the believer confounds and shames the aggressor, creating an opportunity for the hostile person to be reconciled with God. By absorbing undeserved suffering and not retaliating in kind, the disciple destroys the evil inherent in the logic of force. Instead of an endless cycle of bloodshed, fear and recrimination, there is *shalom*, there is peace."

There is nothing sentimental, naïve, meek or mild about Jesus's Way of dealing with enemies. When we recall the concrete historical realities of Roman occupation in first-century Palestine, the shocking and scandalous political implications of Jesus's teaching of nonviolence immediately becomes clear. To grasp the forces now arrayed against Jesus and his fledgling kingdom movement we have only to imagine the fate that would befall a charismatic young man from a rural village in present day Iraq should he travel to Baghdad with a band of followers and begin publicly announcing that God, through him, was about to free the land from the yoke of foreign occupation—and that prominent imams and respected government officials were vipers and hypocrites—*and that the insurgents should lay down their weapons and love their enemies as themselves*. Subversive? Disturbing? Dangerous? Clearly. Yet this was precisely the path that Jesus followed in his perilous journey from Nazareth to Jerusalem.

Whether Jesus's Way of nonviolent enemy love leads to an ethic of strict pacifism, as Yoder convincingly argues, or whether it allows for Christians to engage in what Glen Stassen calls "just peace-making" (preventive or "policing" actions that involve use of force in exceptional cases but remain sociologically and morally distinct from the calculus of war-making[38]), the presumption of the New Testament is therefore overwhelmingly against believers killing their fellow human beings for a "just cause," whether as social revolutionaries (on the "Left") or "just warriors" (on the "Right"). There is not one word in the New Testament to support Linda Damico's claim that Jesus's concern for the liberation of the poor led him to embrace "the violence of the oppressed."[39] We must ponder whether disciples can even legitimately serve as military chaplains insofar as chaplains are not allowed to fully proclaim Jesus's teaching and example to soldiers but must, by the very terms of their entry into the military, ensure that "all efforts . . . maximize a positive impact on the military mission" and "enhance operational readiness and combat effectiveness."[40]

The Things that Are Caesar's

Against the above reading of Jesus's kingdom announcement—as essentially subversive of political authority, involving concern for matters of economic justice and social equality and giving rise to a community of nonviolent nonconformity with power—some scholars have quoted Jesus's aphorism, "Render to Caesar the things that are Caesar's, and to God the things that are God's" (Mark 12:17). According to Geza Vermes, the saying indicates that Jesus was not concerned with the burning political matters of his day but remained a wandering, apolitical sage who only accidentally and somewhat naïvely stumbled into conflict with the Jerusalem authorities.[41] Did not Jesus also say "My kingdom is not of this world"?

Vermes's reading of Jesus as apolitical rustic rabbi fails, however, to account for the historical and narrative contexts for Jesus's words and actions in the Gospels. When Jesus says his kingdom is not *of* this world he does not mean that his kingdom has nothing to do with this world; he means that his kingdom does not derive its tactics, platform or goals *from*

---

38. Stassen and Gushee, *Kingdom Ethics*, 169–74.

39. Damico, *Anarchist Dimension of Liberation Theology*, 173–92.

40. The U.S. military's manuals spell out the duties of the chaplain as a member of the fighting unit in no uncertain terms, suggesting that chaplains who encourage their soldiers to follow Jesus's teaching and example of nonviolence to their enemies will soon be chaplains without jobs. See, for example, "Air Force Policy Directive 52–1: Chaplain Service," available through the Publishing Distribution Office.

41. Vermes, *Passion*, 55.

The Christ of the Fifth Way

any of the competing political movements of his day, and particularly from the zealots: "If my kingdom were of this world *my servants would fight* . . . but my kingdom is not *from* here" (John 18:36 NKJV, emphasis mine). Nor is "Render to Caesar the things that are Caesar's" an abstract teaching about the separation of political and religious matters. The aphorism is Jesus's answer to a specific, historically-inscribed trap devised by a group of Pharisees and Herodians, whose goal is to force Jesus into one of their rival camps.

The trap comes in the form of a question that appears to admit only one of two answers: Should Jews pay the poll tax to Caesar? If Jesus says they should pay the tax, he will have compromised with the Roman occupiers and betrayed his people. If he says that it is not right to pay the tax, he will have openly defied Caesar's authority and be guilty of sedition along the lines of the zealots. But Jesus does not take either path in this false dichotomy. Instead, he deftly transcends and subverts the question.[42] His reply contains irony, non-cooperation, indifference and even scorn.[43] Bring me a denarius, he tells his inquisitors (Mark 12:15), showing that he is not himself in possession of "Lord Mammon" while at the same time forcing his questioners to reveal that they are the compromised bearers of Caesar's image and divine title. Whose image and inscription is this?, Jesus then asks, as if he did not know. So it is the Pharisees and Herodians, not Jesus, who are forced to bear recognition to Caesar in the story. When told that the image is Caesar's (v.16), Jesus at last declares that Caesar can keep his idolatrous scraps of metal: "Render to Caesar the things that Caesar's." But what are the things that truly belong to Caesar? Does Caesar have the right to wage wars, to impoverish nations and to inflict violence on God's people? Not at all, Jesus's listeners would have understood. Lord Caesar has no claim whatsoever on any human being; for human beings, unlike coins, are made *in the image of God*.

But what about the Apostle Paul's statement in Rom 13:1–7 that God has ordained secular rulers as agents of his will, as "avengers" who do "not bear the sword for nothing"? Do Paul's letters—the oldest texts in the New Testament canon—in some way contradict, invalidate or "balance" Jesus's seemingly more radical words and actions in the Gospels, which were written some forty years later? According to Martin Luther, the

---

42. Wright, *Jesus and the Victory of God*, 507.

43. Cullman, *Jesus and the Revolutionaries*, 46–47; Ellul, *Anarchy and Christianity*, 71.

book of Romans is the New Testament's definitive statement on Christian politics, and it shows that we must serve God "inwardly" and the secular authorities "outwardly." "Therefore, should you see that there is a lack of hangmen," Luther wrote in 1523, "and find that you are qualified, you should offer your services and seek the place."[44] Mainline Protestants in the so-called "magisterial tradition" have been offering their services ever since.

Yet Romans 13, Luther failed to see, is part of the same literary unit as Romans 12, which ends with these words: "Never pay back evil for evil to anyone . . . Never take your own revenge, beloved, but leave room for the wrath of God, for it is written, 'Vengeance is mine, I will repay,' says the Lord. 'But if your enemy is hungry, feed him, and if he is thirsty, give him a drink; for in so doing you will heap burning coals on his head.' Do not be overcome by evil, but overcome evil with good" (Rom 12:17–21). Next come the instructions about submitting to earthly authorities. But, lest there be any doubt on the matter, Paul returns to the theme of Christian nonviolence, driving his point home with systematic rigor. First, he instructs believers to render to all their due (13:7). Then he says that believers should owe no one anything except love (13:8). Next he defines what love is: "Love *does no harm to a neighbor*" (13:10 NKJV).

Read carefully, and in historical context, Paul is telling the early Christians in Rome, in the face of increasing persecution by a brutal and tyrannical pagan regime, to assume a nonviolent, non-rebellious stance as their reconciling ministry. He is also telling believers to trust in God's controlling power over history. God can use the secular authorities and their pagan armies for his own redemptive purposes and, ironically, even as instruments of his justice. That is God's power and prerogative. But there is not one word in Romans—or anywhere else in Paul's writings—to suggest that believers should volunteer to serve in Assyrian, Egyptian or Roman legions, or that violence is an acceptable tool for followers of the Way.[45] Quite the opposite, Romans 13 makes clear: Christians are called to a different path. And it is precisely the political character of this path that explains the regularity and persistence of both Roman and Jewish persecution of the Jesus movement during the first three centuries of its growth:

---

44. Luther, "Secular Authority," 374.

45. See Hays, *Moral Vision of the New Testament*, 331.

The Christ of the Fifth Way

Mere belief—acceptance of certain propositional statements—is not enough to elicit such violence. People believe all sorts of odd things and are tolerated. When, however, belief is regarded as an index of subversion, everything changes. The fact of widespread persecution, regarded by both pagans and Christians as the normal state of affairs within a century of the beginnings of Christianity, is powerful evidence of the sort of thing that Christianity was, and was perceived to be.[46]

The Fifth Way

When we strip away the layers of ritual, culture and abstract theology that have accreted to the Gospels over the past two thousand years, we thus find that although Jesus did not fit into any of the rival political categories or ideologies of his day—although he did not "run with the hares or hunt with the hounds" in Wright's words[47]—he was nevertheless deeply, in fact centrally, concerned with politics: with questions of power, money, allegiance and violence, and with the liberation of human beings from all forms of oppression, social and political as well as individual. For Jesus, the things that are God's are not otherworldly things—the heretical, earth-denying claim of the Gnostics—but precisely this-worldly matters—matters of justice, mercy and community. Jesus's political stance, Jacques Ellul and Vernard Eller convincingly argue, may best be described as that of an *anarchist*—not anarchist in the popular sense of advocating destruction of property or the violent overthrow of governments (as in Damico's reading), but in the root sense of the word: *an arche*: no rulers, no dominion but God's alone.[48]

The anarchist dimension of Christian discipleship does not remove, but in many ways heightens, the demands of citizenship in a secular polity since service to God cannot be separated from loving service to humanity, and because violent resistance to "Lord Caesar" is no longer an option. Still, "We must be faithful in our own way," Stanley Hauerwas reminds us, "even if the world understands such faithfulness as disloyalty."[49] A church that does not stand "against the world" in fundamental ways, Yoder points

---

46. Wright, *New Testament and the People of God*, 450.
47. Wright, *Jesus and the Victory of God*, 97.
48. See Ellul, *Anarchy and Christianity*; and Eller, *Christian Anarchy*.
49. Hauerwas, "Church and Liberal Democracy," in *Community of Character*, 85.

out, "has nothing worth saying to and for the world."⁵⁰ Followers of Jesus are not called to defend the ramparts of "liberal democracy," or any other political system or ideology.⁵¹ Nor are they called to create a "Christian nation" in which Christian leaders assume control of the means of violence and power and exercise them for righteous ends. Rather, they are called to incarnate the kingdom of God by modeling an alternative or "remnant" community of economic justice, equality and peace, with Jesus at its center. They are called to bear witness, amid all of the ambiguities and ironies of history, to the "minority report": the good news that Jesus's creative weakness is still God's saving strength.

If true to their calling, followers of Jesus may expect to pay a high price for their political witness and their refusal to play a part in the mechanisms of violence and coercion that lie at the heart of every social order, including the project of American democracy with all of its powers of shock and awe—making "fire come down out of heaven to the earth in the presence of men"—and by its control of the global economy—dictating who is "able to buy or to sell."⁵² They will at times be charged with being unpatriotic, ineffective or irrelevant. Like the Anabaptists during the Protestant Reformation, they may face ridicule, social ostracism and even persecution for their nonconformity with power. In some times and places, they will lose their lives as a result of their obedience to their Master. This is so because the fifth Way, the Way of Jesus, is ultimately the Way of the Cross. "To accept the cross as his destiny, to move toward it and even to provoke it, when he could well have done otherwise, was Jesus' constantly reiterated free choice," writes Yoder. "The cross of Calvary was not a difficult family situation, not a frustration of visions

---

50. Yoder, *Body Politics*, 79.

51. Hauerwas describes the Christian political stance even under democracy as "the posture of the peasant." "The peasant does not seek to become the master, but rather she wants to know how to survive under the power of the master. The peasant, of course, has certain advantages since, as Hegel clearly saw, the peasant must understand the master better than the master can understand herself or himself. The problem with Christian justifications of democracy is not that alleged democratic social orders may not have some advantages, but that the Christian fascination with democracy as 'our' form of government has rendered us defenseless when, for example, that state goes to war." See Hauerwas, *Dispatches From the Front*, 105.

52. I am writing now from out of my heritage as a Seventh-day Adventist. For more on the Adventist reading of America in history and in prophecy, see Morgan, *Adventism and the American Republic*.

The Christ of the Fifth Way

of personal fulfillment, a crushing debt, or a nagging in-law; it was the political, legally-to-be-expected result of a moral clash with the powers ruling his society."[53]

Because the Way of Jesus is the Way of the Cross, the politics of Jesus only fully make sense to those who see the dilemmas of power in "cosmic perspective," to those who are living in the light of Jesus's resurrection as the historical fact upon which the once-hidden meaning of the universe hinges. "As a mundane proverb, 'Turn the other cheek' is simply bad advice," Richard Hays points out. "Such action makes sense only if the God and Father of Jesus Christ actually is the ultimate judge of the world *and* if his will for his people is definitely revealed in Jesus."[54] Put another way, because following Jesus—not simply as a matter of individual spirituality but as a matter of concrete community formation—may involve real sacrifice, suffering and even martyrdom, and because there is no guarantee that this suffering will be politically effective as the world measures effectiveness, there is no reason to follow the Way of Jesus unless the Jesus of history and the Christ of faith are one and the same. If Roman brutality left Jesus buried somewhere in the hills of Palestine alongside all the other messianic revolutionaries of his day, "Let us eat and drink, for tomorrow we die" (1 Cor 15:32). But if Jesus is who the New Testament writers say he is—the suffering Savior of the world who has overcome the principalities and powers and has defeated the final tyranny which is death—then let us "be imitators of God" (Eph 5:1), bearing a more faithful witness to the Way of Jesus and the political shape of his life.

—2007

> I think subversive politics that demands all humans be treated as full & complete humans is reason enough to act & die. I do not need a god to come in the end to make my actions worthwhile.

---

53. Yoder, *Politics of Jesus*, 129.
54. Hays, *Moral Vision of the New Testament*, 338.

4 · *"May Fire Come Out from the Bramble"*

Notes on the Subversion of Political Authority in Israel's Royal History in the Hebrew Bible

[From the conclusion of the Exodus story in the Hebrew Bible continuing through the book of Joshua, Israel has no clear political establishment but is a theocracy in which God rules by either speaking directly to the people or through inspired religious leaders and prophets.] When the twelve tribes continually revert to idolatry, God allows them to be conquered by their heathen neighbors. When they repent, He raises up temporary judges to deliver them. These individuals—including figures such as Ehud, Deborah, and Gideon in the book of Judges—assume no political office or permanent authority but disappear back into the people once their task of deliverance is completed. After leading the Israelites in expelling the Midianites, Gideon, for example, rejects the call from the people to rule over Israel, declaring that rulership belongs to God alone. "Then the men of Israel said to Gideon, 'Rule over us, both you and your son, also your son's son, for you have delivered us from the hand of Midian.' But Gideon said to them, 'I will not rule over you, nor shall my son rule over you; the Lord shall rule over you'" (Judg 8:22–23).

The negative view of political authority expressed by Gideon is perhaps most clearly seen in the book of Judges in the story of Abimelech, Gideon's son by one of his concubines. Abimelech, in a bid to become ruler over Israel, murders Gideon's seventy other sons and has himself crowned king by the men of Shechem and Bethmillo. One of his half brothers, Jotham, however, escapes the massacre and shortly thereafter delivers the following prophetic and politically charged parable to the Israelites: One day all the world's trees decide to anoint a king. They first seek to crown

"May Fire Come Out from the Bramble"

the olive tree, but the olive replies, "Shall I leave my fatness with which God and men are honored, and go to wave over the trees?" (Judg 9:9). Next, the trees turn to the fig, but the fig also replies that it is not his place to "wave over the trees." The vine replies in kind. Finally, the assembly of trees offers kingship to the bramble. The power-hungry bramble accepts with these words: "If in truth you are anointing me as king over you, come and take refuge in my shade; but if not, may fire come out from the bramble and consume the cedars of Lebanon" (v.15).

Abimelech, Jotham declares at the end of this tale, is in fact the bramble—a thorny and treacherous weed absurdly inviting Israel to take refuge in his shade. Having already crowned Abimelech king, though, the people of Shechem must now endure his rule or else face a fiery conflagration. This is the price of submitting to human political authority and kingship in place of divine authority. Those who want to rule are invariably those who are not fit to, while those who put their trust in kings in the end must suffer the destructive might of tyrants.

True to Jotham's prophesy, Shechem soon grows weary of Abimelech's rule and rebels. Abimelech attacks Shechem, whose leaders are forced to take refuge in the inner chamber of the temple of El-berith. Abimelech orders his soldiers to cut down trees and pile them on the roof of the temple. He then sets the wood on fire, killing the rebels inside. Yet the judgment on Shechem proves to be part and the same of Abimelech's own judgment. As he approaches a tower in the city to set it on fire, a woman throws a millstone from above, crushing his skull. As in the stories of Deborah, Delilah, and Jael, it is a "weak" female who thus acts as the agent of divine justice in the biblical narrative, thwarting the designs of powerful and power-craven men.

In the book of Samuel, the Israelites—now as a collective body—nevertheless demand a new political order for Israel based upon pragmatic power calculations rather than prophetic Revelation. Their call for a king is motivated by three concerns. First, the prophet Samuel is growing old and his sons "do not walk in [his] ways" but pursue unjust gain (1 Sam 8:5). Second, the people want to be "like all the nations." Finally, they desire a leader who will "go out before us and fight our battles" (8:20). The cry for a king, then, reflects a legitimate concern for order and social stability. At the same time, it hints of nationalistic and militaristic aspirations beyond the terms of God's covenant, and in fact in defiance of it. "[T]hey have not rejected you," God tells Samuel, "but they have rejected me from being king over them" (1 Sam 8:7). Samuel warns the Israelites what they may expect from a king, and his negative characterization of monarchy serves as a basis for evaluating all of Israel's subsequent rulers, including David and Solomon.

A king, according to Samuel, will build a massive military-industrial-complex and lead the nation into a situation of permanent mobilization for war. He "will take your sons and place them for himself in his chariots. . . . He will appoint for himself commanders of thousands and of fifties, and some to do his plowing and to reap his harvest and to make his weapons of war and equipment for his chariots" (1 Sam 8:11–12). Further, he will inflict oppressive taxes on the people. "He will take a tenth of your seed and of your vineyards. . . . He will take a tenth of your flocks" (8:15, 17). Finally, the kingship will foster meritocracy and hierarchy, with wealth and power—against God's Jubilee prescriptions of regular wealth redistribution—becoming concentrated in the hands of a political elite and their mandarins. "He will take the best of your fields and your vineyards and give them to his officers and to his servants. . . . He will also take your male servants and your female servants and your best young men and your donkeys and use them for his work" (8:14, 16). Power, the prophet Samuel makes clear, will come at a steep cost—but the cost will not be borne by those who wield it.

Despite these dire warnings, the Israelites insist that they must have a king. Saul is crowned and the catastrophe predicted by Samuel begins. In the end, however, it is not Saul who fulfills Samuel's prophetic words. Plagued by madness, jealousy, and paranoia, his reign is too short and too insecure to bear the full fruits of political might. It is, rather, in the reigns of Israel's "great kings"—David and Solomon—that we see Samuel's warnings most fully realized.

As a young shepherd, David first appears in the biblical narrative in a heroic and promising light. The text's positive evaluation of David in his early years reflects the fact that the young David trusts in God's providence rather than his own power or charisma. In contrast to Homer's famous arming scene of Achilles in the *Iliad*, the Hebrew Bible presents an epic *disarming* scene in which David piece by piece removes Saul's heavy battle gear before confronting the giant Goliath with nothing more than a peasant's sling; for "the Lord does not deliver by sword or by spear; for the battle is the Lord's" (1 Sam 17:47a).

"May Fire Come Out from the Bramble"

As David's political power grows in the court of Saul, however, the discerning reader will detect an increasingly unwholesome, calculating, and morally ambiguous quality to his actions. When David at last flees Saul to the city of Gath, it is not the Lord's power that delivers him but his own Odyssean cunning. "So he disguised his sanity before them, and acted insanely in their hands, and scribbled on the doors of the gate, and let his saliva run down his beard" (1 Sam 21:13). David's flight next takes him to the city of Nob where he encounters the priest Ahimelech. Lying about the real nature of his visit, David demands that he and his men be fed consecrated bread from the temple. He then demands that Ahimelech give him a weapon. Ahimelech tells him that Goliath's sword is being kept behind the ephod. "There is none like it; give it to me," David commands (21:9). Armed with the weapon of his one-time Philistine foe, he and his men depart as outlaws into the hills—but not before being spotted by Doeg, an Edomite loyal to the monarchy. The result of David's hasty foray is that Saul massacres the entire city of Nob, "men and women, children and infants; also oxen, donkeys, and sheep he struck with the edge of the sword" (22:19). The blood of these innocents rests in no small part on David, and this perhaps has something to do with the fact that the people of Keilah as well as the Ziphites have no love for him according to the narrative (23:12, 20–21) but are more than willing to hand him over to Saul.

When at last David becomes king of Israel, the text depicts him in a still more unsavory and, ironically, Saul-like light. He dances naked in front of the people, just as Saul once stripped off his cloths in a religious fervor (1 Sam 19:24). [When he goes to war, he does not simply slaughter his enemies according to the requirements of the *ban*: he tortures them to death with games. "He also brought out the people . . . and set them under saws, sharp iron instruments, and iron axes, and made them pass through the brickkiln. And thus he did to all the cities of the sons of Ammon" (2 Sam 12:31a).] *[This part is rarely included!]* At his best—as when he insists that the spoils of war be shared with those who did not fight since it is God's power alone that wins battles (1 Sam 30:23–24)—David the king still recalls David the shepherd, who disdained might and defeated a giant without military weapons. Yet in the final evaluation, David's monarchy proves the dictum that power corrupts and absolute power corrupts absolutely.

At the pinnacle of his reign, David commits adultery with Bathsheba and murders his faithful commander, Uriah. For these sins he is driven into exile by his own son, Absalom, and only narrowly regains the throne

[For some reason Absalom is always painted in a bad light, but I think he is a hero]

47

Anarchy and Apocalypse

after seeing his family divided and Absalom slain. While avoiding total political ruin, David nevertheless ends his days an impotent and vindictive shell of his former self. He goes to battle with the Philistines and is nearly killed by the giant Ishbi-benob (2 Sam 21:16–17). He catches a chill and is attended by the beautiful virgin Abishag to keep warm, but "the king did not know her" (1 Kgs 1:1–4 NKJV). He loses his grip on the administration of the nation and so Solomon must be crowned king while David is still alive (v.39). David's deathbed instructions to Solomon, like those of a Mafia don, advise settling of old scores with political rivals. During Absalom's rebellion, when David was driven out of Jerusalem, a Benjamite named Shimei taunted him for his loss of power. He later promised to spare Shimei's life, but as he lies dying David's thoughts turn to revenge. "I swore to him by the Lord, saying 'I will not put you to death with the sword.' Now therefore, do not let him go unpunished, for you are a wise man; and you will know what you ought to do to him, and you will bring his gray hair down to Sheol with blood" (1 Kgs 2:9). This word—*blood*—is the last to fall from David's lips, and it is a fitting epitaph for his tumultuous and tragically flawed reign.

Yet David, in the biblical narrative and later Jewish tradition, is Israel's "greatest" king, an archetypal figure for messianic hopes. Hebrew Scripture in this way subversively invites us to contemplate the idolatrous and morally corrosive aspects of political power at both individual and national levels—and *even* when placed in the hands of a person of unusual courage, noble intentions, and high character.

Under David's son Solomon, Samuel's vision of an oppressive, militarized state bureaucracy is realized to the last letter. Solomon's first act as monarch is to initiate a bloody purge of any potential political rivals (1 Kings 2). To protect and enhance his power, he assembles an army of 1,400 chariots and 12,000 horsemen—the military machine Samuel so clearly predicted. He hastily forms an alliance with Egypt by marrying Pharaoh's daughter and then, like Pharaoh, institutes state-sponsored slavery—of both foreigners and Hebrews alike—to construct his lavish public works (5:13, 9:15–22). He also uses slave labor in the construction of a stunning new temple complex, which, in both its opulence and its permanence, marks a radical departure from the older, time-oriented faith of Israel during its desert wanderings, to the space-oriented, centralized religion of imperium.

"May Fire Come Out from the Bramble"

The proverbial opulence of Solomon's temple is conspicuously dwarfed, however, by the opulence of his own royal palace. The House of God measures 60 by 20 by 30 cubits and takes seven years to complete (1 Kgs 6:2, 38). Solomon's palace, according to the biblical narrative, measures 100 by 50 by 30 cubits and takes thirteen years to complete (1 Kgs 7:1–8). He then builds an equally grandiose palace for his Egyptian wife while filling his court with a menagerie of "ivory and apes and peacocks" (1 Kgs 10:22)—all the trappings of conspicuous and concentrated wealth. Solomon's decadence is perhaps most evident, though, in his insatiable sexual appetite, which includes a retinue of 1,000 heathen wives and concubines, who ultimately lead him down a path of idolatry from which he never recovers.

Solomon's political achievement, Walter Brueggemann concludes, involves three dimensions that both Moses before and the major prophets after would radically oppose: unprecedented affluence, consumption, and satiation; oppressive foreign and domestic social policy as a way of sustaining the royal political economy; and the establishment of a controlled, static religion closely aligned with the goals of the state, administered by compliant priests, and impervious to prophetic criticism.[1] When Jeroboam confronts Solomon with a prophetic rebuke from God, Solomon attempts to have him murdered, forcing Jeroboam to flee into exile in Egypt (1 Kgs 11:40). Under Solomon's reign, the land of Israel has thus become a land of slavery, while the land of Israel's former enslavement under the pharaohs has become the last refuge of those who would speak truth to power. The replacement of divine rule by human political authority—in the span of three kings, as the biblical narrative presents it—has led to a catastrophic reversal of the Exodus story.

The nation after Solomon is divided into two warring houses: the House of Israel and the House of Judah. The kings of the House of Israel are presented by the biblical writers as corrupt and evil without exception; every one of their reigns—from Jeroboam until Hoshea and the Assyrian conquest—is marked by intrigue, violence, and idolatry. Meanwhile, the rulers of the House of Judah—from Rehoboam until Zedekiah and the exile in Babylon—are depicted as being either corrupt, oppressive, or ineffectual with a single exception: Josiah, who rediscovers a lost book of the Law and launches a massive war against idolatry, although too late to

---

1. Brueggemann, *Prophetic Imagination*, 26–32.

Anarchy and Apocalypse

save Israel from the accumulated sins of previous leaders (and particularly of Manassah, who caused God to vow to "abandon the remnant of my inheritance"). There are six other kings of Judah—Asa, Jehoshaphat, Joash, Amaziah, Azariah, and Jotham—who, according to the text, "did right in the eyes of the Lord." But each of these monarchs fails to remove the high places, allowing idolatry to persist with increasingly dire consequences for the nation as a whole. Hezekiah, the only other leader beside Josiah whose rule is not characterized by idolatry, corruption, and bloodshed, meanwhile foolishly shows off Israel's treasures to a delegation of Babylonians, causing the prophet Isaiah to predict Judah's exile at the hand of Nebuchadnezzar (2 Kgs 20:12–19).

It is possible, of course, to find contrary passages in the royal histories describing the "glories" of David's and Solomon's reigns. These will be pointed to by some as evidence that the biblical writers held a more positive view of political authority than I have suggested. But once we overcome the fundamentalist temptation to pin all meaning to single texts and learn to pay attention to the trajectory of the narrative *as narrative*—to the way these texts function within the arc of the larger Jewish *story*—we quickly discover that the Hebrew Bible contains an imaginative and prophetic vision of God's reign over history that radically subverts all human pretensions to political power and control. "The presentation is so systematic," Jacques Ellul writes, "that some modern historians suggest that the accounts were written by antimonarchists and partisans."[2] What is even more remarkable, these texts (as well as the still more politically charged books of the Hebrew prophets such as Isaiah, Amos, and Jeremiah) were edited and circulated by rabbis among the people while some of the kings in question were still alive—and they were accepted by the people as divine revelation, as the Word of God. The God of Israel, Ellul points out, "is thus presented as himself an enemy of royal power and the state."[3] Religious leaders who support the kings are meanwhile seen as sycophantic "false prophets" and systematically excluded from the canon, so that "false prophet" in Hebrew Scripture is virtually synonymous with "one who supports the king."

—2002

2. Ellul, *Anarchy and Christianity*, 50.
3. Ibid., 50–51.

5 · *Anarchy and Apocalypse*

The Radical Social Ethics of an American Religion

I

Most radical dissenters in American history have, at a fundamental level, been deeply committed to America itself as "a city on a hill," a nation of unique promise and destiny. Ralph Waldo Emerson, Henry David Thoreau, and Mark Twain all criticized the United States for betraying its highest ideals, but they never questioned the sanctity or permanence of the founding vision, or the reality of a peculiar "American Dream." Freedom and democracy might undergo temporary setbacks, these reformers believed, but by appealing to the principles enshrined in the Constitution, as well as the character of the American people, all such obstacles might be overcome. It was in this spirit that one of the greatest radicals of the twentieth century, Martin Luther King Jr., organized his Southern Christian Leadership Conference. He took as the organization's motto: "To save the soul of America." "America is essentially a dream, a dream as yet unfulfilled," King declared in a speech at Lincoln University, Pennsylvania, in 1961. "Now, more than ever before, America is challenged to bring her noble dream into reality, and those who are working to implement the American dream are the true saviors of democracy."[1]

The early Seventh-day Adventists—the nineteenth-century pioneers of the peculiar and little-known denomination in which I was raised and continue to find Christian community—were clearly political dissenters in this patriotic tradition. The United States, they believed, embodied freedom as no other nation in the world. Founded upon the twin pillars of

---

1. King, "American Dream," in *A Testament of Hope*, 208.

civil and religious liberty, the American experiment could not fail so long as the country remained true to its Republican and Protestant heritage. When Sabbatarian Adventists agitated against slavery or opposed Sunday legislation for a "theocratic ideal," they did so precisely by appealing to America's own best virtues. "We might expect a millennium indeed," wrote John N. Loughborough in response to the optimistic post-millenial doctrines of other denominations, "if only America would live up to its professions."[2] By forcefully highlighting these professions, Adventists saw themselves as the true defenders of America's original greatness. Their dissent from American society was in fact a mark of their loyalty to it.

At the same time, Adventist eschatology led the fledgling movement to a more radical and systematic critique of the United States than that of Thoreau, King, or other great prophetic voices in the American tradition. The Republic could not fail so long as it remained faithful to the libertarian principles upon which it was founded, it was true. Yet according to their reading of the apocalyptic books of Daniel and Revelation, the fact that America *would* eventually fail was a foregone conclusion. No nationalistic project could replace the divine plan to redeem humanity once and for all. The creedalism and intolerance of the emerging Protestant empire—intent upon a new union of church and state—coupled with the social injustice in the economic order built upon the backs of slaves, revealed the seeds of corruption eating at the heart of the American experiment. The United States, early Adventists declared in language very similar to the language of religiously motivated Garrisonian abolitionists, was none other than the beast of Revelation 13, a morally contradictory amalgamation of dragon and lamb-like qualities. Even the best government in human history, it turned out, had feet of clay. Where King and other optimistic reformers believed that freedom and justice would unfold and expand until the American Dream was at last realized as a historical reality, Adventist apocalyptic insisted that America's precious freedoms would narrow and erode until the dream finally turned into a nightmare.

The dissenting impulse of Adventists in the first seventy years of the church's history in this regard had less in common with Thoreau or King's radicalism than with the politics of another, far more unsettling American libertarian. As unlikely as it may first appear, the social ethics of Ellen White, Joseph Bates, A. T. Jones, and other early Adventists

2. Morgan, *Adventism and the American Republic*, 19.

finds dramatic resonance in the ideas of none other than Noam Chomsky. Chomsky's anarchist critique of America may seem a far cry from the patriotic stance of many current Seventh-day Adventists, who today tend to identify closely with the politics of conservative evangelical Christianity. But the latent connections between Adventist apocalyptic and anarchist thinking cannot be ignored. I will first examine some of the anarchist elements in early Adventist thought and then discuss the religious roots of Noam Chomsky's own political views.

II

To begin, Ellen White, like anarchist political theorists, saw hierarchical political and social structures as standing in fundamental opposition to liberty and genuine human community. In the case of White, the focus fell primarily on religious hierarchies, typified in her view by the Roman Catholic Church, which barter freedom of conscience for a kind of order and security. The theme of her major work on theodicy and eschatology, *The Great Controversy*, published in 1888, is, however, that of an essentially political insurrection in Heaven. Satan has called into question the justice of God's government, which rests upon free and spontaneous love. He has attempted to set in its place a new order based upon the laws of merit and power. The world, then, is a proving ground for these two conflicting principles at work. Human history is in fact the stage for a "trial" of cosmic significance: a trial of the law of power versus the law of love. All political systems, founded as they are upon calculations of self-interest, merit, and coercive force, therefore tend toward the demonic and the tyrannical. Because "realism"—including bourgeois state capitalism as in the United States—leaves little place for relationships between peoples or nations based upon unmerited love or grace, the power and dominion of the state must ultimately stand as an idolatrous parody of God's kingdom and authority.

The attitude of the early Adventists toward the U.S. government was therefore deeply subversive to say the least, although this subversive strain exists somewhat uneasily alongside other more patriotic declarations. While generally avoiding direct confrontation with the "beast" and seeking to exemplify Christian love to its officials, nineteenth-century Adventists nevertheless urged defiance of the Supreme Court's Fugitive

Anarchy and Apocalypse

Slave Law, refused to bear arms in the military, shunned public office and partisan politics, fought in the courts against compulsory public schooling, thundered against American imperialism in the Spanish-American War, and on occasion refused to salute the flag or say the pledge of allegiance. Biblical apocalyptic led the movement to what they took to be an apolitical stance. Yet this very apoliticism on closer examination proves to contain the seeds of a potentially potent and anarchic challenge to the powers that be—not anarchic in the sense of advocating disorder, chaos, or violent revolution but in the sense of challenging the false order of the state that rests upon violence and the disordering of human lives.

Beyond calling into question the power of the state, the Adventist pioneers likewise rejected the brutality and coercion implicit in the capitalist order. Their outlook might thus be described as libertarian socialist, with concern for individual freedom not leading to simplistic allegiance to market values, as may be found among many conservative libertarians, but to a vision of distributive justice grounded in a theology of the Sabbath Jubilee. Under the topics of "wealth" and "poverty," the *Index of the Writings of Ellen White* contains nearly twenty pages of citations. Many of these statements are in the spirit of the following passage from *Patriarchs and Prophets*:

> The principles [of Sabbath economics] which God has enjoined, would prevent the terrible evils that in all ages have resulted from the oppression of the rich toward the poor and the suspicion and hatred of the poor toward the rich. While they might hinder the amassing of great wealth and the indulgence of unbounded luxury, they would prevent the consequent ignorance and degradation of tens of thousands whose ill-paid servitude is required to build up these colossal fortunes. They would bring a peaceful solution to those problems that now threaten to fill the world with anarchy and bloodshed.[3]

In the same chapter, White writes that there will always be a diversity of "temporal blessings" and that those who urge an absolute leveling of material possessions are mistaken in their zeal. But in opposition to the capitalistic values of regnant American Protestantism, she sees economic justice in terms of a well-known anarchist principle: the principle of solidarity. "We are all woven together in a great web of humanity," White declares. "The law of mutual dependence runs through all classes of so-

---

3. White, *Patriarchs and Prophets*, 536.

ciety." The monopolistic accumulation of wealth by elite classes tends to "demoralize society and open the door to crimes of every description," while God's laws "were designed to promote social equality."[4] Concretely, these convictions resulted in early Adventists adopting a denominational pay structure based not upon market values but upon the belief that even at Adventist hospitals and universities doctors and administrators should not earn significantly higher wages than the persons who cleaned their offices.

Much of White's writing on the topic of education thus deals with the need for dignity in labor and the problems of alienation and exploitation associated with the division of society into managerial and menial classes. "We are not to do brain work and stop there, or make physical exertions and stop there," she writes with regard to Adventist colleges and universities, "but we are to make the very best use of the various parts composing the human machinery—brain, bone, and muscle, body, head, and heart."[5] Adventist communities, and Adventist schools in particular, were to model a kind of radical egalitarianism based upon the life and teachings of Jesus. "At the feet of Jesus," White declares, all "distinctions are forgotten. The rich and the poor, the learned and the ignorant, meet together, with no thought of caste or worldly preeminence."[6] In practice, this meant that at Adventist schools honorific titles would not be used for teachers with advanced degrees. Students, teachers, and administrators would meanwhile work side by side as full partners in the quest for truth, both in and out of the classroom. Hence, for example, at the third biennial session of the Australasian Union Conference held at Avondale College in Australia in 1899, delegates at the end of each day of meetings removed their coats and spent two hours performing manual labor alongside students.

Through the nineteenth century and into the early part of the twentieth, we therefore find a quiet but unmistakable current of anarchist thinking and practice among Seventh-day Adventists. Believers do not align themselves with any particular political party or movement but remain staunchly, sometimes stridently, pacifist, anti-nationalist, anti-creedal, and anti-capitalist. They reject political and religious authoritarianism

---

4. Ibid., 534–35.
5. White, "Counsel on Food," in *Manuscript Releases*, 221.
6. White, *Desire of Ages*, 437.

Anarchy and Apocalypse

and any union of "throne and alter." And they organize themselves in small fellowships and companies that largely disavow participation in the activities of the state while periodically agitating against the government when they perceive that vital liberties are at stake. Like their Anabaptist forebears of the Radical Reformation, Adventists see themselves in fundamental tension with society and the state. And ultimately, they see themselves in confrontation with the United States in particular, the dragon of John's apocalypse who "doeth great wonders, so that he maketh fire come down from heaven on the earth, and deceiveth them that dwell on the earth by the means of those miracles" (Rev 13:13–14).

III

With the preceding outline of Adventism's anarchist connections in mind, we may now examine the religious and apocalyptic roots of Noam Chomsky's particular anarchism. "If one were to seek a single leading idea within the anarchist tradition," Chomsky writes, "it should, I believe, be that expressed by [nineteenth-century Russian anarchist thinker Mikhail] Bakunin":

> I am a fanatic lover of liberty, considering it as the unique condition under which intelligence, dignity and human happiness can develop and grow; not the purely formal liberty conceded, measured out and regulated by the State, an eternal lie which in reality represents nothing more than the privilege of some founded on the slavery of the rest.... No, I mean the only kind of liberty that is worthy of the name, liberty that consists in the full development of all the material, intellectual and moral powers that are latent in each person; liberty that recognizes no restrictions other than those determined by the laws of our own individual nature, which cannot properly be regarded as restrictions since these laws are not imposed by any outside legislator beside or above us, but are immanent and inherent, forming the very basis of our material, intellectual and moral being—they do not limit us but are the real and immediate conditions of our freedom.[7]

Bakunin's statement illustrates that there can be no absolute identification between classical anarchist and early Adventist thought; Ellen

---

7. Bakunin as cited in Chomsky, "Notes on Anarchism," in *For Reasons of State*, 374–75.

White would strenuously reject his assertion that there is no "legislator above us" as well as his claim that human liberty can be ultimately grounded in humanity's own "immanent" properties. Nevertheless, there are several striking parallels between early Adventist and anarchist visions. Both are concerned with the holistic development of the person; both reject the view that authentic human freedom can be guaranteed by the liberal state; and both seek the emancipation of individuals from hierarchical ecclesial and political structures, which they see as destroying liberty of conscious. Like the early Adventists, many contemporary anarchist thinkers, including Chomsky, have also focused their critique of power on the United States in particular.

According to Chomsky—considered the founder of modern linguistics and famously described by *The New York Times* as "arguably the most important intellectual alive"—the true story of America and its institutions of power is not one of ever-expanding freedom and liberty, but one of greed, imperial aggression, violence, injustice, and contempt for humanity, all masked by sophisticated mechanisms of propaganda and thought control. "We are hardly the first power in history to combine material interests, great technological capacity, and an utter disregard for the suffering and misery of the lower orders," Chomsky writes. "The long tradition of naiveté and self-righteousness that disfigures our intellectual history, however, must serve as a warning to the Third World, if such a warning is needed, as to how much our protestations of sincerity and benign intent are to be interpreted."[8] The United States, in Chomsky's analysis, is therefore indeed unique among world empires in its ability to speak as a lamb while acting as a dragon.

In opposition to the American system with its values of unfettered individualism and capitalist accumulation, Chomsky envisions a society that would offer no privileged role to professional intellectuals or other elite groups. Those whose labor primarily involves knowledge "would have no special opportunity to manage society, to gain any position of power and prestige by virtue of this special training and talent."[9] Nor, in such an anarchist state, would individuals work exclusively with their minds but would participate with their hands in other forms of action essential to the good of the community—ideas that trace back to Chomsky's personal

---

8. Chomsky, "Responsibility of Intellectuals," in *Chomsky Reader*, 126.
9. Chomsky, "Interview with James Peck," in *Chomsky Reader*, 21.

experience working on an Israeli kibbutz in the 1950s. Anarchism for Chomsky, then, does not imply lack of order but a different kind of order based upon radically communitarian values as well as unassailable personal freedoms. Unlike Marx and other optimistic socialist and anarchist thinkers, Chomsky harbors few utopian illusions that the Good Society will be realized in the foreseeable future. Still, he believes, human beings, as free moral agents, can make a difference, and must try to make a difference, whether or not they succeed. "[W]hile I expect that any worthwhile cause will achieve at best very limited success, and will quite probably largely fail, nevertheless there are accomplishments that give great satisfaction, however small they may be in the face of what one would like to see," he writes. Concerned, marginal, and desperate people—"that's the milieu I want to be a part of." "[E]ver since I had any political awareness, I've felt either alone or part of a tiny minority." "I was always on the side of the losers."[10]

If it is not apparent to readers by now, these are not the words of an ivory tower intellectual, a mere social theorist, or even a political activist in any straightforward sense. These are the words, I would argue, of a Hebrew prophet. This is not surprising considering Chomsky's personal background. Both of his parents were Russian Jewish emigrants who fled Czarist rule to America in 1913, and both eventually became teachers of Hebrew language at a religious school of the Mikveh Israel congregation in Philadelphia. His father was a renowned scholar of medieval Hebrew grammar, and Chomsky was raised steeped in the Hebrew Bible and Jewish history and culture. He would later be immersed in the new ideas of various anarchist, libertarian, and Marxist writers in New York in the 1940s. But in fact, Chomsky biographer Robert Barsky points out, these radical thinkers were not presenting new ideas at all: they were reviving the old Jewish Messianic faith and the well known categories of biblical apocalyptic. "The libertarian movement used a new terminology for ancient Jewish ideas, which were near to the hearts of these young Jews."[11] Its leaders were driven by an unflagging desire to conceive an alternative social order and to not accept the injustice of the prevailing order, with its powerful and revered institutions, as either permanent or necessary. They were not afraid to hold the American empire accountable to higher

---

10. Ibid., 13–14, 55; Chomsky as cited in Barsky, *Noam Chomsky*, 24.

11. Rocker as cited in Barksy, *Noam Chomsky*, 24.

Anarchy and Apocalypse

standards of freedom and equality than state-capitalism allows. And they refused to compromise their dissent, even at great personal cost: they were jailed for "un-American" activities; they were expelled from universities and teaching posts; they were marginalized by their colleagues and peers; they were harassed and intimidated by the government; and they died in relative obscurity to the rest of society.

Yet it is groups such as these, along with Spanish peasant anarchists in the 1930s and radical Anabaptist Christians like the Quakers, that Chomsky most identifies with—movements he sees in a long line of champions for freedom and liberty stretching most dramatically back to the Bible itself. There have always been two kinds of people, he writes: the commissars and the dissidents. In the Jewish faith:

> The intellectuals who gained respect and honour were those who were condemned centuries later as the false prophets—the courtiers, the commissars. Those who came to be honoured much later as the Prophets received rather different treatment at the time. They told the truth about things that matter ranging from geopolitical analysis to moral values, and suffered the punishment that is meted out with no slight consistency to those who commit the sin of honesty and integrity.[12]

[margin note: we all choose a side]

In reply to a letter I sent him, Chomsky wrote to me that from his early childhood he has been deeply moved by the prophets, and particularly his favorite, Amos of Tekoa. A consideration of Amos's indictment of Israel reveals a number of striking similarities to Chomky's own analysis of the United States. In the time of Amos, the Kingdom of Israel had reached its zenith in material power and economic prosperity. The wealth and splendor of the North, however, was built upon corruption, exploitation, violence, and slavery. Hence, declared Amos, the nation's ritual piety, its scrupulous Sabbath observance, was little more than a noxious affront to God. To those who "trample the heads of the poor into the dust of the earth," the Lord vowed only lamentation and sackcloth. Insatiable and arrogant empire building was an affront to the moral law, and the prophet was filled with disgust for the military boots, for the mercenary hands dipped in blood. Not surprisingly, Amos's invectives pitted him against the political and religious establishment and the naïve and vulgar patriotism of his day. These corrupt minions of power rejected his mes-

---

12. Chomsky, *Powers and Prospects*, 62.

Anarchy and Apocalypse

sage as intolerable and irresponsible and ordered him to "never prophesy at Bethal" again "for it is the king's sanctuary." Because he had sided with the poor and downtrodden rather than with the state, he was played for a fool and reviled as a traitor.

IV

It may seem to some readers that an anarchist reading of early Seventh-day Adventism is anachronistic and untenable since the word *anarchism* came into general usage at a later time. Many anarchists have also been violently opposed to religion and Christianity in particular, taking as their watchword the slogan, "No gods, no masters." Further, while Adventists may have questioned political and religious authoritarianism in others, the authoritarian, institutional, and hierarchical drive *within* Adventism cannot be denied. Does this not invalidate any similarities between anarchy and apocalyptic? Both Adventism and anarcho-syndicalism, I have shown, however, share similar concerns and affinities, and have intellectual roots in the same biblical sources. The anarchist current within Christianity has often been weak or nonexistent. But the striking fact is that there *is* a Christian anarchism, and that this anarchism has much to do with the apocalyptic beliefs of early Seventh-day Adventists.

The question therefore arises: what happened to the Adventist church? The Anabaptist ethos of the pioneers has been lost in nearly every area, but particularly with regard to the U.S. government and military. Instead of decrying American imperialism in prophetic language as evidence of the beast at work as they once did in response to America's annexing of the Philippines, church leaders today decorate their offices with patriotic bunting and the national flag, praying all the while for God's blessings on the U.S. military machine. There was a time when loyalty to the American Dream meant not unthinking compliance with power, but vigorous activism and radical dissent. That day is gone.

Still, it may be the spirit of early Adventism is not entirely lost but merely submerged, waiting to be recovered. It might not be too late for Adventists to return to their firm foundation in anarcho-syndicalism. The question hinges on whether Adventists can find new ways of thinking about biblical apocalyptic that are also somehow old and true ways. They might begin by revisiting Daniel and Revelation, but also Amos,

Anarchy and Apocalypse

Isaiah, and the other prophets of the Hebrew Bible. They might mine the writings of Ellen White and the Adventist founders for clues as to what an apocalyptic social ethic would look like. And they might read Noam Chomsky—a prophetic thinker who, unlike the early Adventists, is skeptical of the "American Dream" from its founding, but who, like the Adventist pioneers, refuses to invest the American empire with idolatrous prerogatives or permanency.

—2002

> I think I may agree more with Chomsky than I do with E. White...

6 · *The Death of a Peace Church*

The Seventh-day Adventist Church was founded by New England pacifists with intellectual and spiritual roots in the Radical or Anabaptist Reformation. In the first sixty years of the movement's history—from its organization in 1863 until the death of its prophetess, Ellen White, in 1915—Adventism may thus be seen as part of the same tradition of social and political dissent that gave rise to Quakers, Mennonites, and other religious communities committed to the ethics of nonviolence.

This commitment was both formally stated and rigorously practiced by early Adventists, many of whom believed that even touching a weapon was sinful. On May 17, 1865, the *Review and Herald* published a General Conference resolution "as a truthful representation of the views held by us from the beginning of our existence as a people, relative to bearing arms." The document—composed in the aftermath of a war that had caused many abolitionists to abandon their earlier pacifism—affirmed a legitimate role for the civil government, but declared that Adventists, as a people, are "compelled to decline all participation in acts of war and bloodshed as being inconsistent with the duties enjoined upon us by our divine Master toward our enemies and toward all mankind."[1]

During the Spanish-American War of 1898–1899, Adventists thus emerged as outspoken critics of America's imperial foreign policy. In opposition to other prominent churches that embraced the war as a Christianizing and civilizing campaign, they pointed to the glaring inconsistency of linking the cross with militarism of any sort. "Christian love demands that its possessor shall not make war at all. 'Put up again they sword into his place,' is the word of the Author of Christianity, the embodiment of Christian love," thundered former army sergeant A. T.

---

1. "General Conference Resolutions," in Morgan, *Peacemaking Remnant*, 96–97.

The Death of a Peace Church

Jones. "Christianity is one thing; war is another, and far different thing. Christians are one sort of people; warriors are another and different sort of people."[2] Percy Magan's *The Peril of the Republic,* rushed to print in 1899, similarly denounced American imperialism in the Philippines as mere "colonial greed and rapacious lust." Better, Magan argued, "for a few missionaries to lose their lives at the hands of heathen savages than for heathen savages to lose their lives at the hands of those calling themselves Christians."[3] The Adventist commitment to nonviolence during this period of the church's history was based not primarily upon concern for personal moral purity, but upon a systematic critique of America's revered institutions of power. According to the Adventist apocalyptic reading of the books of Daniel and Revelation, the United States was none other than the beast of Revelation 13, an aggressive kingdom or empire bestriding the world at the climax of earth's history, speaking like a lamb while acting like a dragon. ← still is, more so than ever!

From Ellen White's death in 1915 on, however, the Anabaptist ethos of the early church rapidly eroded. This was true in matters of ecclesiastical authority and biblical hermeneutics, but particularly with regard to the military and bearing arms. During World War I, a minority of German Adventists parted ways with the church after being sharply criticized by church officials for resisting the Kaiser's draft. Meanwhile, in the United States, the Adventist commitment to not taking life remained largely intact; yet church leaders increasingly described Adventists not as conscientious objectors but as "conscientious cooperators." The consensus of the new generation was that it was no longer the church's role to question the rightness of military adventures or foreign policy so long as Adventist soldiers were allowed to continue in their peculiar commitment to Sabbath observance. ← a milk-toast position

It was in this spirit of patriotic cooperation with the government that the Adventist Medical Cadet Corp was created in 1942. The Corp sought to prove that good Adventists were also "good Americans," eager and willing to serve in the military, albeit in noncombatant roles. The Corp thus helped to instill in a generation of young Adventists a love for drill and bivouac, and the belief that it is honorable to serve power for the sake of order. Unfortunately, these lessons could not be confined to one

this is amazing! (in an horrifying sense)

2. Jones and Smith, "A Novel Christian Duty," in Morgan, *Peacemaking Remnant,* 102–4.

3. Morgan, *Adventism and the American Republic,* 69.

Anarchy and Apocalypse

side of the Atlantic. During World War II Adventists proudly answered the call to duty in the United States, but also, disconcertingly, in Nazi Germany. While Protestant leaders of other denominations resisted fascism at considerable cost, there was no Adventist "Confessing Church," and up to the outbreak of the war Adventists even in the United States spoke of Hitler in positive terms as a fellow vegetarian concerned with matters of bodily hygiene.

Whereas Adventist complicity in the Nazi onslaught, as well as the horrors of the Allied bombing campaign, might have sparked a recommitment to the nonviolent principles of the church's pioneers, Adventists from the 1950s on generally saw World War II as a vindication of violence for a just cause. The idea that loyalty to God and loyalty to the military were fully compatible became powerfully entrenched in the minds of many Adventists, particularly in North America. Pockets of believers in Europe, such as Germany's Reformed Adventists, retained the older ethics of nonviolence; and Russia's True and Free Adventists heroically resisted Soviet totalitarianism in defense of freedom and human rights. But these pacifists—whose convictions placed them firmly in the tradition of the church's founders—were disavowed and marginalized by presiding church officials. With a burgeoning network of health and educational institutions and ambitious evangelistic campaigns around the world, maintaining good relations with government authorities now took precedence over prophetic and politically dangerous brands of dissent.

With more and more Adventist chaplains rising in military rank, the church was also already too deeply invested in the military as an institution to seriously question the logic of violence, or the rightness of American foreign policies abroad. The title of the Adventist chaplaincy's newsletter, *For God and Country*, revealed just how far pietism and patriotism had come to be wedded in the thinking of church leaders—and how far Adventists had come since Magan's *Peril of the Republic*.

By the time of the Vietnam War the Adventist position had thus fragmented into incoherency. Some Adventists evaded the draft, others entered as noncombatant medics, and others avoided direct military action by volunteering as human guinea pigs in Project White Coat—a research program with links to the U.S. biological weapons laboratories at Fort Detrick, Maryland. During the war in Vietnam, significant numbers of Adventists, encouraged by church officials to perform their patriotic duty according to "the dictates of their conscience," also picked up guns

The Death of a Peace Church

and, for the first time, began to kill according to the dictates of government planners.

In view of the vociferous Adventist response to the Spanish-American war, the silence of the church during the war in Indochina—and particularly the silence of those chaplains closest to the unfolding catastrophe—marked a stunning reversal of Adventism's historic identity, from fearless prophetic agitators to acquiescent mandarins of the state. Religious leaders of other faiths, such as Martin Luther King Jr., Thomas Merton, and Abraham Joshua Heschel, decried the war in unequivocal language. But through the carpet-bombing with napalm of hundreds of thousands of defenseless villagers, through the countless acts of brutality and depredation against unarmed civilians, through the dumping of millions of gallons of arsenic-based herbicides on Vietnamese crops and people—through all of this Adventists spoke not a word. In a tragically ironic twist, even as America acted increasingly like the beast Adventists had long proclaimed it to be, the prophetic movement proved an increasingly timid page at the dragon's side.

In the post-Vietnam era, thousands of Adventists voluntarily joined the U.S. armed forces as full combatants. Adventist chaplains were recruited to minister to the "spiritual" needs of these fighters (now understood as something entirely unrelated to matters of social and political witness) "without passing judgment," which in turn encouraged more Adventists to enlist. With large numbers of Adventists on active duty, it is not surprising that there was not a murmur of disapproval from the church in the 1970s and 1980s as the U.S. military abetted brutal Latin American juntas in the slaying of tens of thousands of impoverished peasants calling for land reform—many of them Christians who first heard about the Sabbath Jubilee from socially conscious Catholic priests.

During the 1990s and at the start of the twenty-first century, the collapse of the historic Adventist ethic of nonviolence became apparent in other embarrassing ways. Early Adventist apocalyptic had led the movement to reject all acts of violence and bloodshed, but in Waco, Texas, in 1993 one-time Adventists played out a new and violent apocalyptic nightmare on a compound bristling with weapons. In 1994, significant numbers of Adventist Hutus in Rwanda participated in the genocide of their Tutsi countrymen, including an estimated 10,000 Seventh-day Adventists. Through the 1990s—as Buddhist Nobel Peace Prize winner Aung San Suu Kyi attracted world attention in her nonviolent struggle

65

Anarchy and Apocalypse

against Burma's brutal military dictatorship—thousands of ethnic Karen Adventists, whose great-grandparents had been evangelized by legendary missionary Eric B. Hare, engaged in a campaign of insurgency warfare against the Burmese army with the goal of creating an autonomous Karen nation. And in 2002, rival militias comprised largely of Adventists fought for control of the government of the Solomon Islands.

Yet while Adventists were quick to dismiss these events as tragic aberrations in the faith, they did not pause to consider the church's involvement with more devastating forms of violence sanctified by the state. In 2002, several Adventist students from Oakwood College were arrested on charges of gunrunning between New York and Alabama. But through the 1990s the church saw no reason to disavow the voting records of Adventism's two most prominent gunrunners: Republican United States Congressmen Roscoe Bartlett of Maryland and Bob Stump of Arizona, who each collected hefty sums from the National Rifle Association and military manufacturing lobbyists for helping to grease weapons sales at home and abroad.

The September 2001 terrorist attacks in the United States seemed to mark the final denouement of Seventh-day Adventism as a prophetic movement that could not be co-opted by nationalistic crusades. Amid the many heartfelt and sincere expressions of grief following the tragedy, churches from coast to coast reflexively wrapped themselves in the flag, no different from the rest of evangelical America. Sligo Church in Washington, DC (one of the denomination's flagship churches attended by many prominent church officials), featured a Veteran's Day service in which a military honor guard marched down the center aisle with bolt-action rifles gripped to their chests. Near the end of the American bombing campaign in Afghanistan, the General Conference organized a special weekend to honor the U.S. military and send care packages overseas—not care packages to the afflicted Afghanis, but stuffed animals to U.S. bomber crews stationed at Diego Garcia Air Force Base in the Pacific Ocean. Little thought was given by the planners of the event to the history of American intervention in the Middle East, the relationship between U.S. military and economic policy, or the estimated 3,400 Afghani civilians killed by U.S. bombs—several hundred more innocent people than perished on September 11. Where Adventists once venerated those Protestant martyrs who died rather than betray their religious convictions, they would now honor soldiers who kill at the bidding of politicians. As President

The Death of a Peace Church

George W. Bush promised to take his war against America's enemies to far-flung corners of the globe, one thing was certain: many Adventists would soon be shipping off to exotic lands, not as missionaries, but as warriors, assault rifles in hand.

—2003

7 · William Lloyd Garrison and the Problem of Constitutional Evil

On August 6, 1824, William Lloyd Garrison, not yet twenty years old, penned a letter to the Salem *Gazette* opposing John Quincy Adams's bid for the presidency and endorsing the candidacy of a dedicated Georgian, United States Senator William Crawford. There is no mention in the document of the slavery issue and no hint that the young Garrison viewed the Constitution as anything less than a triumph of the founding fathers. The "high and exalted character" of the elections proved the Federalist Party "worthy of its great leader, the immortal WASHINGTON," and spread "vigor and strength throughout the political fabric of our constitution and government," Garrison wrote.[1] "It is peculiarly gratifying, too," he declared, "to observe the dignified course pursued generally by the few *sentinels of freedom*, who advocate and uphold those principles, which were promulgated by the Father of his Country, and sanctioned by JAY and HAMILTON, and AMES, with a host of other distinguished patriots." Garrison went on to stress the civic duty of voting, arguing that although no citizen was legally required to support any of the presidential candidates, reason "dictates that we should" so as not to upset "the peace of the Union." Federalists should make pragmatic political choices, he wrote, and not squander their votes on ideal but unlikely candidates. "Though we might prefer men of our own principles, yet as their chance of success would be next to impossibility, it would be the climax of folly for us to throw away that influence, which we can now exercise, in order to support a hopeless experiment." Within five years, however, Garrison would publicly condemn the Constitution as an "unjust" text and demand

---

1. Garrison, "To the Editor of the Salem *Gazette*," in *Letters of William Lloyd Garrison, Volume I*, 27–28.

the "overthrow" of its slavery provisions. By 1833, he would sharpen his critique of America's founding document, describing it as a "compact . . . dripping with blood." From the early 1840s until the outbreak of the Civil War, Garrison would call in uncompromising language for the North to secede from the South, and would urge his fellow abolitionists, as a matter of Christian duty, to refuse to vote in national elections. How and why did Garrison's thinking about the Constitution and the Union change so dramatically? What was the political and constitutional logic behind his radical critique of America's political order?

In what follows I will trace the development of Garrison's politics of disunion, showing how the abolitionist leader's ideas evolved over time and exploring the underlying pragmatism of Garrisonian thinking. Flawed and problematic as Garrison's politics were, I will argue, disunionism was based upon a realistic reading of the Constitution as a proslavery document and a plausible calculation of what was necessary to end slavery without war. Garrison did more to force the issue of slavery into public debate and to galvanize the nation around the slavery issue than any other individual. There are ways to work to advance the good society, he demonstrated in the process, that do not involve compromise with massive injustice *or* sacrifice of nonviolent principles.

"The Right to Remonstrate": From Newburyport Partisan to Boston Agitator

Garrison's loyalty to the Federalist cause sharply declined after he moved to Boston in 1826 to edit the *National Philanthropist*, a failing temperance newspaper published beneath the masthead: "Moderate Drinking is the Downhill Road to Intemperance and Drunkenness."[2] Garrison had acquired skills as a writer while working as an apprentice for the *Herald* newspaper in the town of Newburyport, publishing editorials supporting partisan Federalist positions under the pseudonym "Aristides" (after the Athenian senator known as "the just"). In Boston, though, he directly encountered the clannish rivalries and prejudices of New England's merchant elites. He tried to speak during a Federalist caucus at Faneuil Hall but was shunned by the city's genteel aristocrats. A critic in the *Boston Courier* disdainfully described an "impudent" young man who nobody

2. Mayer, *All on Fir*, 49–50.

knew taking the floor and speaking without control from notes crammed into his hat.[3] Blocked from entering New England's elite circles of power, which had no tolerance for independent voices arising from the lower classes, Garrison, a devout Christian, therefore devoted himself to religiously based social reform movements and to the denunciation of political parties that turned matters of principle into issues of mere expedience. Under the influence of a Quaker harness maker named Benjamin Lundy, who had learned the printing trade in order to excoriate the evils of slavery and who became a friend and mentor of Garrison's in 1828, Garrison became particularly sensitized to the cause of abolition.

On July 4, 1829, Garrison delivered an address at Park Street Church to the American Colonization Society that marked the beginning of his public critique of the Constitution and sounded the major themes that would animate his politics over the next three decades. The text deserves a careful reading both for its theoretical and its historical significance. Garrison began—to the great embarrassment of the committee that had invited the young editor to speak in honor of America's independence—by declaring that American political life, founded on noble principles, was now "rotten to the core," corrupted by "unprincipled jugglers," who like Esau in the Bible had sold their "birthright for office."[4] He then proceeded with iconoclastic audacity to describe "another evil" that was "a gangrene preying on our vitals—an earthquake rumbling under our feet." The free states, Garrison said, were "constitutionally involved in the guilt of slavery, by adhering to a compact that sanctions it." It was their "right to remonstrate against its continuance," however, and "their duty to assist in its overthrow." To make sure his audience did not miss the subversive point he was making, he heaped scorn on politicians "who turn pale, retreat and surrender, at a talismanic threat to dissolve the Union." If "we are always to remain shackled by unjust Constitutional provisions, when the emergency that imposed them has long since passed away; if we must share in the guilt and danger of destroying the bodies and souls of men, *as the price of our Union*; if the slave States will haughtily spurn our assistance, and refuse to consult the general welfare; then the fault is not ours if a separation eventually takes place."

3. Ibid., 51.

4. Garrison, "Address to the Colonization Society." Online: http://teachingamerican history.org/library/index.asp?document=562.

William Lloyd Garrison and the Problem of Constitutional Evil

While Garrison did not hesitate to place moral principle above constitutional loyalty, he nevertheless suggested that free states were duty-bound to agitate against slavery precisely for the sake of preserving the integrity of the Union. Slavery was "a business in which, as members of one great family, we have a common interest."[5] It was the responsibility of Americans to "watch over the interests of the whole country, without reference to territorial divisions." Garrison appealed to majoritarian and common sense principles to support his case, pointing out that the white population in the North was nearly double the size of the white population in the South. Counting slaves as property but also as members of the population for purposes of congressional representation was politically spurious, even if constitutionally mandated, and deprived Northerners of "their just influence in the councils of the nation." Garrison was not himself committed to disunion, these statements make clear, but was rather assuming the role of public prophet, warning an America still fatalistically and almost universally resigned to slavery of an impending national catastrophe growing out of flaws and internal contradictions in its founding text. The solution was moral and political pressure from an aroused citizenry, leading to constitutional amendment. "There must be a beginning, and now is a propitious time—perhaps the last opportunity that will be granted us by a long-suffering God." Abolitionists would not abandon the law or engage in tactics of violence, for "we have not the right, and I trust not the disposition, to use coercive measures." But the Constitution could not prevent antislavery activists from striving to "alleviate the condition of the slave" or from applying moral pressures to "operate upon public sentiment," pressing the Constitution in the direction of liberty as far as they were able. "Moral influence, when in vigorous exercise," Garrison declared, "is irresistible."

At the heart of Garrison's Park Street address was the radical claim, still denied by almost all antislavery New Englanders, that blacks and whites were by nature *fully* equal and that there was only one human race. The slave's "claims for redress are as strong as those of any Americans could be in a similar condition," Garrison proclaimed.[6] In pointed opposition to the colonization platform of the organization he was addressing, he called for the emancipation and education of black people in order to "elevate" them "to a rank with the white" as "intelligent and peaceable

5. Ibid.
6. Ibid.

citizens." He urged his white listeners to imaginatively place themselves in the situation of blacks and declared that if they did there would be no more talk of "constitutional limitations" but "patriotic assemblies would congregate at the corners of every street." The success of the antislavery movement, Wendell Phillips would later say, lay in Garrison's forgetting that he was white and looking at constitutional questions from the perspective of a Negro.[7]

At the heart of the speech also lay Garrison's commitment to the Declaration of Independence as the most primary and authoritative statement of the American political experiment. The Declaration was a document of "sublime indignation," he asserted, by which the Constitution itself ought to be continually judged. Unlike Frederick Douglas, however, who by 1851 would argue on linguistic and aspirational grounds that the Declaration and the Constitution were fully in harmony against slavery, Garrison interpreted the Constitution, as a matter of historical fact and political realism, as a compromise with human bondage that betrayed the republican and revolutionary spirit of 1776.[8] The Declaration, he concluded, pointed toward the need for a second revolution—a nonviolent revolution but a revolution nonetheless—that would spread the promise of equality to all persons, regardless of their color. In Park Street Church, Henry Mayer writes, Garrison did nothing less than rewrite the Declaration of Independence to include African-Americans. The speech was "the most forthright and extensive statement of American egalitarian principles written between the Declaration of Independence and the Gettysburg Address."[9]

"A Compact Dripping with Blood": Garrison Sharpens His Critique

Over the next several years, Garrison repeated and sharpened the ideas of his Park Street address in the pages of *The Liberator* (the abolitionist paper he began in 1831), in vigorously argued letters to friends and foes alike, and in antislavery speeches delivered to small but growing abolitionist groups across New England. Using religious ideas as his lever, he attacked church and state alike for betraying the founding ideals of the

---

7. Nelson, ed., *Documents of Upheaval*, xv.
8. See Douglas, *Frederick Douglas Papers*, 228–29.
9. Mayer, *All on Fire*, 67.

republic and the basic precepts of Christian morality. The Park Street speech was barely noted in the press at the time Garrison delivered it, but his campaign soon attracted the attention—and the wrath—of politicians, clergymen, judges, and proslavery militants in both the North and the South. Garrison thrived on controversy, though, invariably responding to his opponents with still greater provocations, no matter the dangers to his reputation or person. Garrison's critique of the Constitution through the early to mid-1830s reflected his general tendency to escalate confrontation and to stake out ever more radical positions in order to continually shift the political center in the direction of emancipation.[10] "Yes, I recognize the compact," he wrote in 1833, "but with feelings of shame and indignation."[11] The founders had "trampled beneath their own feet their own solemn and heaven attested declaration, that all men are created equal." But they "had no lawful power to bind themselves, or their posterity, for one hour—for one moment—by such an unholy alliance." The Constitution "was so framed as to guarantee the legal possession of slaves" and was therefore "dripping ... with human blood."

Garrison's increasingly harsh indictment of the Constitution as a proslavery document must be seen in the context of increasingly violent actions by proslavery forces intent on silencing abolitionist speech. When defenders of slavery resorted to "feathers, brickbats, and all sorts of argumentative missiles" in the name of protecting the Constitution and the Union, they exposed the moral ambiguities of America's political order, and the ultimate incoherence of republican values with a constitutionalism that condoned slavery.[12] Garrison experienced firsthand the perils of free speech, even for abolitionists in Yankee Boston, the cradle of the Revolution. On August 21, 1835, a proslavery mob, incited by Boston merchants angry at Garrison for declines in their West Indian trade, gathered at Faneuil Hall to seize the editor during one of his talks to a group of abolitionists. Garrison walked into the angry crowd and, he recounted in *The Liberator*, delivered the following announcement:

> Gentlemen, perhaps you are not aware that this is a meeting of the Boston *Female* Anti-Slavery Society, called and intended exclu-

10. Mayer, "William Lloyd Garrison," 106.

11. Garrison, "To the Editor of the London *Patriot*," in *Letters of William Lloyd Garrison, Volume I*, 249.

12. Garrison, "To Peleg Sprague," in *Letters of William Lloyd Garrison, Volume I*, 518.

Anarchy and Apocalypse

> sively for ladies, and those only who have been invited to address them ... If *gentlemen* ... any of you are *ladies*—in disguise—why, only appraise me of the fact, give me your names, and I will introduce you to the rest of your sex, and you can take seats among them accordingly.[13]

Garrison's actions, while demonstrating his courage, did not prove a model of conflict resolution. By the end of his talk, the mob outside had grown to several hundred men chanting: "Garrison! Garrison! We must have Garrison!" The editor narrowly escaped being lynched with the aid of a constable after fleeing from one building to another through Boston's narrow streets, the mob in close pursuit. He was locked in a Boston jail for his own safety.

The violence of the proslavery mobs allowed Garrison to heap still greater scorn on the slavery clauses in the Constitution. At the same time, it enabled him to appeal, ironically and not entirely consistently, to the Constitution's authority. As long as abolitionists' efforts to "modify or repeal the present compact" by moral persuasion were met with coercive force, as long as there was "neither liberty of speech nor of the press, on the subject of oppression, in a large portion of our country," the Constitution was clearly not being upheld by its alleged defenders, he pointed out.[14] The "constitution is trampled under foot, 'a blurred and tattered parchment,' by a slaveholding faction and their northern adherents!" he wrote. The "Union itself gives no protection to those who dare to believe, ay, to say, that slaveholding is in all cases a sin against God, and war upon mankind!" "[T]he sacred right of petition is struck down to the earth by the despotic arm of Congress ... anarchy prevails in all parts of the land, mob-law against the advocates of liberty being sanctioned and administered by judges, lawyers, and the officers of government, both in church and state."[15]

Garrison thus presented his brand of challenging the Constitution and the "despotic arm of Congress" as the paradoxical mark of his loyalty to the Union. The abolitionists, in contrast to proslavery reactionaries who claimed to be defending the law, remained committed to nonviolent and essentially legal processes to overturn the Constitution's unjust

---

13. As cited in Nelson, ed., *Documents of Upheaval*, 87.
14. Garrison, "To the Editor of the London *Patriot*," 251.
15. Garrison, "To Joseph Kimball," in *Letters of William Lloyd Garrison, Volume II*, 286.

slavery provisions. "Give us fair-play, secure us the right of discussion, the freedom of speech," said Hinton Helper, "and we will settle the difficulty at the ballot box, not the battleground—by force of reason, not force of arms."[16] Several months after the Boston riot, Garrison expressed once again his hope that conscientious citizens would be able to "blot out that bloody stain" of slavery by "procuring an amendment to our national Constitution—that part of it which is wet with human blood, which requires the free states to send back into bondage those who escape from the lash and the chain."[17]

The logic of Garrison's critique was nevertheless pushing him in an increasingly radical, if not anarchic, direction. Garrison continued to insist that abolitionists "proposed to do nothing, that was repugnant either to the letter or the spirit of the U.S. Constitution" but to fight only armed with "the incendiary spirit of truth."[18] The forces of freedom, he declared, held three fundamental principles: 1) "A man is a man, and not a chattel"; 2) "Hence, he cannot be the property of another"; and 3) "Hence, that which makes him a chattel is unnatural, monstrous and unholy, and ought to be immediately destroyed." Until these three statements were shown to be false, he wrote to proslavery advocate Peleg Sprague, "you can never prove them to be either slightly or imminently dangerous to the constitution of the Union."[19] The argument, however, was already showing its strains. If it was the Constitution itself that was responsible for making human beings into chattel, did it not follow, by Garrisonian reasoning, that the Constitution "ought to be immediately destroyed," not merely amended through a legislative process? And had not Garrison already declared that the Union was forged through this very compact, "dripping with human blood"?

"Our Country is the World": The Constitution and the Kingdom

Garrison was moving away from the ideal of constitutionalism in still another, more profound and more unsettling, way. The principle of democratic majoritarianism, to which he had appealed in his 1829 Park

16. As cited in Graber, *Dred Scott and the Problem of Constitutional Evil*, 233.
17. Garrison, "To Thomas Shipley," in *Letters of William Lloyd Garrison, Volume I*, 584.
18. Garrison, "To Peleg Sprague," 519, 536.
19. Ibid., 536.

Street address before the American Colonization Society, gave way in Garrison's thinking after the "mobocracy" of Boston to the idea of a moral "remnant" that by its courageous actions might save the whole—even, if necessary, against the wishes of the majority, albeit through the force of moral suasion alone. "[T]he success of any great moral enterprise does not depend upon numbers," he wrote in September of 1835.[20] "Slavery will be overthrown before a majority of all the people shall have called voluntarily and on the score of principle, for its abolition." Garrison increasingly rested his hopes not on changing the minds of compromising politicians but on shaming Christians into bearing "a united testimony" against slavery. Revival in the churches would cause the system to fall, "not because they embrace a majority of the people, for they are in a lean minority, but because their example is mightier than an armed host."

Where Madison and the other framers of the Constitution had sought to construct an ideal political system based on the principle of counterbalancing vice against vice, self-interest against self-interest, Garrison sought to transform society by resurrecting virtue and transforming slaveholders' hearts. "Political economy is too weak to contend against the giant passions which sustain slavery," he asserted. "So is the principle of fear." The antislavery movement could only succeed by making abolition "a great religious enterprise."[21] HolyScripture, then, was the abolitionist's chief weapon against the sin of human bondage. It was only through the alternative political grammar of the Kingdom of God, and the agitation of a vanguard of committed Christian activists, that America might be saved. The Bible, Garrison came to believe, contained all of the laws and political principles necessary to govern humankind.[22]

The idea that the nation ought to be judged, and even governed, according to Scripture and Christian teachings alone might be terrifying to contemporary civil libertarians concerned with protecting individual rights against conservative religious forces through constitutional and legal guarantees. But it is important to grasp what the politics of "the Kingdom" actually implied for Garrison. The politics of the Kingdom, in subversive opposition to the politics of the state, demanded a repudiation of violence, coercion, and imperialism, and an ethic of strict pacifism

---

20. Ibid., 519.

21. Garrison, "To the Abolitionists of the United States," in *Letters of William Lloyd Garrison, Volume II*, 567.

22. Van Deburg, "William Lloyd Garrison and the 'Pro-Slavery Priesthood,'" 228.

and respect for individual liberty of conscience that would bear faithful witness to the life of Jesus. Garrisonian abolitionists were not attempting to maneuver like-minded politicians into positions of power where they might exercise the coercive tools of the state for righteous ends. Instead, they were counter-posing what they saw as the only true and effective government—God's government of freedom and love—against all human systems of domination and control. Their experience with lynch-mob brutality and massive injustice in the antebellum order led them to conclude that "government" was in fact a manifestation of anarchy, while what others branded anarchism was the foundation of true law. Slavery, government, and violence, Lewis Perry writes, were closely linked in abolitionist thinking. "All were sinful invasions of God's prerogatives; all tried to set one man between another man and his rightful ruler."[23] Over and against the Constitution, the abolitionists offered a millenarian vision of a transformed society in which there were no intermediaries—priestly or political—between the individual's conscience and divine rule. Garrison recognized the necessity of the law and coercion by the state to constrain "the wicked" in the interim. But he refused to allow that this should fundamentally alter abolitionist tactics or goals. "What then? Shall we, *as Christians*, applaud and do homage to human government? Or shall we not rather lay the axe at the root of the tree, and attempt to destroy both the cause and the consequence together?"[24]

Between 1835 and 1840, Garrison "bombarded the American religious establishment with every epithet that was not too vile to include in a speech or a newspaper article."[25] The Methodist Episcopal Church was "a cage of unclean birds, and synagogue of Satan." The Baptist Board of Foreign Missions was a pawn in the hands of cowardly "mansteakers." He always sounded "like a newly discovered chapter of Ezekiel," one minister recalled.[26] Not all abolitionists, however, were willing to follow Garrison into what he later wryly referred to as the "kingdom of Disunion."[27] By 1839, Garrisonian antinomianism had led to a bitter feud in the Anti-Slavery Association, openly fought on the pages of *The Liberator*. James

23. Perry, *Radical Abolitionism*, 59.
24. Garrison as cited in Kraditor, *Means and Ends in American Abolitionism*, 81.
25. Van Deburg, "William Lloyd Garrison and the 'Pro-Slavery Priesthood,'" 232.
26. Mayer, *All on Fire*, 326.
27. Garrison, "To Elizabeth Pease," in *Letters of William Lloyd Garrison, Volume III*, 624.

Anarchy and Apocalypse

G. Birney attacked those who refused to vote as a matter of religious duty as a "No-Government sect," while Garrison defended nonresistance even at the polls as a legitimate Christian witness to the anarchy of the state. "[T]his country will be purified and renovated, in exact proportion to the prevalence of the great conservative doctrines of non-resistance!" Garrison declared.[28] "This may seem, to many, absurd, paradoxical, impossible," yet "our 'pro-government' brethren have obtained new views of duty at the polls, and are indebted for their awakened consciences and rectified vision to the despised and calumniated non-resistants." Garrison assumed that slavery would ultimately be dismantled through voting by the masses, if not by bloody slave rebellions. But he also believed that principled refusal to vote by the *moral minority* was necessary to uphold the "impassable gulf" between church and state, which was being compromised in sinister ways by "Priests [who] have become politicians."[29] "Now the pulpit and the religious press are teeming with homilies upon the religious duty of going to the polls—upon the divine institution of human government," Garrison lamented, but the government remained "hideously defective," bearing "little or no resemblance to the gospel of Christ." A conscientious and public refusal to engage in voting by a faithful remnant might therefore make clear the true radicalism of the gospel, and might also affect a more dramatic change in society than mere electioneering.

The debate centered, it is no small irony, on whether the Anti-Slavery Association's *Constitution* permitted members to abstain from voting. The document stated that all members would "endeavor, in a constitutional way, to influence Congress" to abolish slavery. In Birney's construction, the only way to "influence" Congress in a "constitutional way" was through the elective franchise.[30] But Garrison insisted (with his usual energy) that "those who conscientiously abstain from voting may be constitutionally members ... BECAUSE THE DUTY OF VOTING IS A POINT WHICH THE CONSTITUTION [of the Anti-Slavery Association] HAS LEFT UNDECIDED."[31] The organization might endorse positions on any

---

28. Garrison, "Reply to James G. Barney," in Nelson, ed., *Documents of Upheaval*, 159.

29. Ibid., 159–60.

30. Birney, "Of the Constitution of the American A.S. Society as Connected with the 'No-Government' Question," in Nelson, ed., *Documents of Upheaval*, 154–58.

31. Garrison, "To the Abolitionists of Massachusetts," in *Letters of William Lloyd Garrison, Volume II*, 512.

number of tactical questions, he argued, but it had "no power to bind the conscience or coerce the will of members acting in their individual capacity, and no right to preclude from membership those who refuse to go with the majority." Garrison proved unable, however, to preserve the abolitionist union. In 1840, Birney and others acrimoniously seceded from the Anti-Slavery Society to form the Liberty Party, for voting abolitionists only, with the goal of ending slavery through electoral channels. Garrison at first emphasized the underlying unity of the different abolitionist groups—voters and non-voters alike—and their shared commitment to the "ONE OBJECT" that mattered most: ending slavery.[32]

Later, as racist and anti-woman's suffrage elements of the voting abolitionists' platforms emerged, he would castigate the Liberty Party in savage language as an "insidious" and "dangerous" foe to "genuine anti-slavery"—despite, or perhaps because of, the fact that it successfully advanced an anti-slavery agenda in elections across New England.[33] The political and ideological fissures that emerged in the 1840s within the abolitionist movement thus illustrated the basic problem that has plagued all millenarian movements—and all constitutional experiments—throughout history: flawed human natures and conflicting visions of the good, even among persons with shared political goals.

Yet if the weakness of Garrisonian millenarianism lay in its overly optimistic assessment of its own moral purity and in its dogmatic assertions of the power of moral persuasion, its strength was its articulation of the dark side of the Union. It dared to see the Union through the lens of biblical realism and in the light of a luminous vision of universal human rights. Garrison embraced a distinctly Christian presence in public life, but in contrast to later Evangelical political activists he strenuously rejected the myth of America as a "city on a hill," a nation uniquely favored by God or divinely guided in history. Instead, he blasted the idolatry of nationalistic enthusiasm and uncritical flag-waving of every sort, emphasizing the insignificance and impermanence of America and the Constitution in cosmic perspective, forcing his listeners and readers to continually reorient their ultimate political allegiances. "We imagine, and are constantly taught to believe, that our flight, like a strong angel's, is onward and upward, without pause, without weariness," Garrison wrote. "Like ancient

32. Ibid., 512.
33. Garrison, "To the Liberator," in *Letters of William Lloyd Garrison, Volume III*, 245; and Laurie, *Beyond Garrison*.

Edom, our habitation is high; we have exalted ourselves as an eagle, and set our habitation among the stars; and we are saying in the pride of our hearts, 'Who shall bring us down to the ground?'"[34] But "what are the United States in the estimation of the Almighty?" he asked in the radical spirit of the Hebrew prophets Isaiah and Jeremiah. "Do their dimensions excite his wonder? Is he impressed by their arts and sciences, their enterprise and opulence, their politics and religion, their high pretensions and solemn protestations?" The failure of America to uphold individual liberties, its brutal enslavement of persons of color, its duplicitous annexation of Texas for purposes of extending slavery, its unabashed celebration of economic and military might—all revealed that the country was in fact a profoundly *pagan* nation, not a new Promised Land but a new Egypt. "It has been confidently asserted, that if our experiment fail, all hope will be taken from the earth," Garrison noted. But America was not the last best hope of the world. "[C]ome what may of this republic," God "will maintain the cause of the afflicted and the right of the poor, and . . . will deliver the oppressed out of the land of the spoiler." If "our destruction is to come, I am ready to say, 'O give thanks unto the Lord, for he is good; for his mercy endureth forever. To him that overthrew Pharaoh and his hosts; for his *mercy* endureth forever!'"[35]

The politics of the Kingdom were thus a transcendent and universal, not a sectarian, politics. Garrisonian abolitionists refused to participate in the normal mechanisms of government and staked out ever more radical positions not because they rejected social responsibility in order to maintain clean hands, as the voices of gradualism charged, but because they were committed to a higher vision of human community than antebellum laws or conventions could afford.

Pragmatism and the Case for Disunion

But was Garrison *effective*? Did the "politics of the Kingdom" *work*? "Garrison may have awakened the conscience of some Northerners," Bruce Laurie has argued, but "he also led his followers into something of a moral dead end. He steadfastly insisted that the answer to the moral

---

34. Garrison, "To Elizabeth Pease," in *Letters of William Lloyd Garrison, Volume II*, 325.

35. Ibid., 326.

cleansing of individual souls was more moral cleansing, a seemingly endless pursuit of self-purification that mistook the avoidance of politics for progress even as political abolitionism eclipsed his own movement."[36] Garrison, more than any other single individual, may have awakened—and polarized—the nation on the slavery issue. But his nonresistant tactics failed to bring an end to slavery or to avert the violence he abhorred. His eldest son would ultimately enlist, against Garrison's pleadings, to fight with the all-black 55th Massachusetts Regiment.[37]

Laurie's in many ways trenchant critique does not do justice, however, to the underlying *pragmatism* of Garrisonian abolitionism. While Garrison's radical Protestantism led him to emphasize the moral autonomy of the individual and the necessity of conversion before collective action, and although his religious thinking steadily evolved in the direction of a form of Christian anarchism similar to that of the Society of Friends, Garrison's only gage of individual piety nevertheless remained practical obedience in the realm of human social relations. He freely entered into political alliances with Unitarians, spiritualists, socialists, and others deemed "heretics" by the establishment churches and parties so long as they shared his commitment to immediate emancipation. This was hardly the stance of a moralist concerned only with an "endless pursuit of self-purification." Nor did Garrison's refusal to vote amount to an "avoidance of politics," as the Boston mob in 1835 well understood. Garrison and his followers interpreted slavery through the lens of Scripture, but they also interpreted Scripture through the lens of Enlightenment *reason* and *republicanism*.[38] There was a complex interplay of religious idealism and political realism, then, in Garrisonian thinking. Garrison's brand of agitation—including his call for disunion from the early 1840s until the outbreak of the Civil War—emerged from his thoroughly plausible reading of the Constitution as a proslavery document, and from his pragmatic calculation of what was politically necessary in the light of this fact to achieve emancipation without war. If anything, history suggests, Garrison may have been right: the only way to end slavery without war *might* have been through Northern secession from the South, leading to the South's economic isolation, containment, and collapse from within.

36. Laurie, *Beyond Garrison*, 5.

37. Garrison, "To George Thompson Garrison," in *Letters of William Lloyd Garrison, Volume V*, 160.

38. McInerney, *Fortunate Heirs of Freedom*, 64.

Anarchy and Apocalypse

Garrison, we saw, was already attracted to the idea of disunion when he delivered his 1829 Park Street address, in which he argued that the North was being held hostage by the South's "talismanic threat" of secession and proclaimed his support for disunion *if* it proved the only way to end slavery. He expressed alarm in 1833 at the fact that Northern troops were "constitutionally bound" to suppress any black rebellion in the South and urged the North to "give them fair warning when we intend to leave them to their fate."[39] By 1837, his Christian pacifism led him to repudiate allegiance to all forceful governments, even apart from the slavery issue.[40] Still, Garrison long believed that the South was too dependent on the North to act out its threats of secession.[41] Disunion, then, was not at first a positive prescription to the problem of slavery in Garrison's thinking but a way to call the South's bluff. During the early 1840s, however, disunion took on a new importance for Garrison, Wendell Phillips, and others in the Anti-Slavery Society. Separation from the South was no longer merely a political threat, a hypothetical possibility, or a prophetic warning but an essential goal toward which all abolitionists should vigorously strive. Suppression of free speech in the South—and in Congress after the Gag Rule of 1837, which was provoked by Garrisonian publications and petitions—the annexation of Texas by "piratical seizure," and especially the Supreme Court's ruling in support of fugitive slave laws in the 1842 case of *Prigg v. Pennsylvania* all convinced Garrison that disunion was the only way to cut the Gordian knot of constitutional evil.

On May 31, 1844, the New England Anti-Slavery Convention formally endorsed a disunion platform by a vote of 250 to 24. A new banner was unveiled for the organization bearing the image of an eagle preying upon the Constitution. The banner's inscription read: "Immediate and Unconditional Emancipation" and "No Union with Slaveholders." Garrison delivered an impassioned speech at the meeting to thunderous applause. "We are not traitors to a free Constitution," he cried, "our principles are the only ones on which a free government can stand."[42] The Society, he would write later that year, "has 'passed the Rubicon', in regard

---

39. Garrison, *Documents of Upheaval*, 43.
40. Kraditor, *Means and Ends in American Abolitionism*, 196.
41. Garrison, "To Samuel J. May," in *Letters of William Lloyd Garrison, Volume IV*, 4.
42. As cited in Mayer, *All On Fire*, 328.

William Lloyd Garrison and the Problem of Constitutional Evil

to this blood-cemented Union."[43] In 1847, Garrison wrote that it was "the first duty of every citizen . . . to devote himself to the destruction of the Union and the Constitution, which have already shipwrecked the experiment of civil liberty . . . assured that out of the wreck, we may confidently expect a State which will unfold, in noble proportion, the principles of the Declaration of Independence."[44]

Disunion was a pragmatic and plausible political position in antebellum America in at least four ways. First (Garrison's frequently intemperate rhetoric notwithstanding), the theory of disunion was based on a thoroughly sober analysis of the Constitution as the foundation of a system of government that was structurally biased toward the preservation of slavery. The historical record, Mark Graber has shown, supports this pessimistic reading more than those aspirational readings—including Lysander Spooner's, Frederick Douglas's after 1850, and Abraham Lincoln's[45]—which sought to enlist the Constitution in the cause of emancipation. "Every national institution was sensitive to Southern interests," Graber points out: "Proslavery policies were handed down in numerous areas . . . Congress refused to discuss abolitionist petitions. The national executive ordered postmasters not to deliver abolitionist mailings . . . The Supreme Court decided most important constitutional questions in favor of slaveholding interests . . . Every federal justice who adjudicated a fugitive slave case upheld the Fugitive Slave Acts of 1793 and 1850."[46] It simply was not true that the framers intended to put slavery on a course to ultimate extinction. What they intended, and achieved, was to forge a bisectional consensus that would guarantee protection to the South from overweening Northern interference. The fact that Garrison rejected this bargain as both morally and politically untenable did not mean that he failed to understand its nature. Rather, his radical politics emerged from the realistic and practical view that slavery would not be dismantled through

---

43. Garrison, "To Henry C. Wright," in *Letters of William Lloyd Garrison, Volume III*, 265.

44. Garrison, "To Elizabeth Pease," in *Letters of William Lloyd Garrison, Volume III*, 478.

45. See, for example, Lysander Spooner's 1860 tract, *The Unconstitutionality of Slavery*, in which he argued on complex semantic grounds that the Constitution was opposed to human bondage. Online: http://www.lysanderspooner.org/UnconstitutionalityOfSlaveryContents.htm.

46. Graber, *Dred Scott and the Problem of Constitutional Evil*, 149.

a constitutionalism based on complex wordplay that ignored structural realities and half a century of proslavery decisions by the courts. Even if the document *could* be read as Spooner, the Liberty Party, and others desired as a matter of purely verbal logic, "such a construction is not to be tolerated *against the wishes of either party*," neither of which, as a matter of political fact, were willing to countenance constitutional amendments to end slavery.[47] The Constitution, in Garrison's view, was proslavery for the plain reason that this was how it had been understood and interpreted by those in power and had been accepted by most Americans. Even Lincoln, we should not forget, vowed to uphold the Constitution by vigorously enforcing fugitive slave laws.

The theory of disunion was also pragmatic in that it was calculated not simply to absolve the North of its guilt in the sin of slavery but to bring about slavery's end in the quickest possible way without war, leading to the reestablishment of the Union under a reconstructed Constitution. In Garrison's view, "without the existing Union the South would be compelled, for self preservation, and from necessity, speedily to liberate all her bondmen; and thus the overthrow of this blood-stained compact would lead to the formation of a 'solemn league and covenant' between all the States, based upon universal freedom, with no root of bitterness to poison our cup."[48] Disunion "is not to leave the slaves to the mercy of their masters: it is to withdraw from those masters all the resources and instrumentalities now furnished to them by the North, without which they are powerless." It was a matter of "physical and geographical necessity, that separation will inevitably give the death blow to the whole slave system."[49] These statements suggest that Garrison's strategic thinking was similar to Lincoln's during the 1850s. Lincoln described slavery by way of analogy as a cancer that could not be surgically removed without endangering the patient's life. It was best, then, not to attempt to abolish slavery through force but to encircle and *quarantine* it, allowing it to whither and die of its own internal contradictions.[50] Garrisonian disunionism, while betraying a naïve optimism as to the speed and ease with which slavery would

---

47. As cited in Mayer, *All On Fire*, 326.

48. Garrison, "To James Miller McKin," in *Letters of William Lloyd Garrison, Volume IV*, 408.

49. Garrison, "To the Pennsylvania Anti-Slavery Society," in *Letters of William Lloyd Garrison, Volume IV*, 496.

50. Kane, *The Politics of Moral Capital*, 56.

collapse, was based on the same pragmatic reasoning, though Garrison took one further and entirely realistic step in the argument: slavery would whither away *if* the South faced a more aggressive sanction regime than the Constitution would ever allow. As long as the Union remained, there could be no effective "quarantine" of the South as Lincoln imagined. Only disunion would permit Northerners to freely aid and abet fugitive slaves. Only disunion would lead to the South's complete economic isolation and stagnation. Only disunion would produce the conditions necessary for reform from within the South while avoiding a path of violence that, even if successful, would "poison" the Union with "bitterness" and hatred for years to come.

Third, Garrison's call for disunion may be viewed as being itself a pragmatic tactic of moral provocation, self-consciously designed to shift the center of political debate in the antebellum order. "To propose a dissolution of the Union is the best way of holding up such a mirror to the national mind, as makes it to see its own deformity," he wrote. "Disunion startles a man to thought. It takes a lazy abolitionist by the throat, and thunders in his ear, '*Thou* art the slaveholder.'"[51] By staking out the most radical and "fanatical" positions on issues of slavery, women's suffrage, and religious liberty, Garrison repeatedly—and effectively—forced Americans to reevaluate what was truly radical and what were matters of common sense and basic humanity. Most citizens would never identify themselves as Garrisonian abolitionists, yet his "extreme" call for disunion as a political outsider enabled individuals within the mainstream of American political thought to embrace more forthright antislavery positions.

The culmination of Garrison's moral provocation and agitation against the Constitution occurred on July 4, 1854, during an abolitionist rally in the town of Framingham, sixteen miles west of Boston. Sojourner Truth and Wendell Phillips delivered stirring anti-slavery speeches and Henry David Thoreau appealed to the crowd to put their humanity before their patriotism. "The law will never make men free," Thoreau said, "it is men who have got to make the law free." Citizens ought "to be men first . . . and Americans only at a late and convenient hour."[52] Garrison at last took the stage. He spoke in melancholy language about the violence and evil he saw in the world, and about the failure of the republic to live up

---

51. Kraditor, *Means and Ends in American Abolitionism*, 212.
52. As cited in Mayer, *All On Fire*, 444.

Anarchy and Apocalypse

to its ideals. He was compelled, he said, to publicly act out his innermost convictions. At this moment, he held aloft a copy of the Fugitive Slave Law, lit a match, and set the paper on fire. As the law burned, Garrison cried out to the audience, "And let all the people say 'Amen'!" A great shout of *Amens* echoed through the grove. But Garrison was not yet done. Holding up a copy of the Constitution he declared that the document was "the source and parent of the other atrocities." Striking another match, Garrison stirred the crowd with the cry, "So perish all compromises with tyranny!"[53] As the Constitution burst into flame, Garrison repeated his evangelist's call: "And let all the people say, 'Amen.'" The crowd erupted into a roar of applause, although some observers, accustomed to Garrison's anti-constitutional *rhetoric*, now hissed at his disturbing and prophetic *act* of dissent.

The war came. How did Garrison respond? Garrison's complex, if not precarious, pragmatism may finally be seen in the fact that when the North rejected his politics of nonviolence and disunion and the South rejected his repeated appeals to conscience and seceded from the Union, he embraced the use of force as a necessary evil to end slavery and, ironically, *to uphold the Constitution*. Several years before Lincoln's election, in the aftermath of John Brown's 1857 raid on Harpers Ferry, Garrison declared that, "Whenever there is a contest between the oppressed and the oppressor—the weapons being equal between the parties—God knows my heart must be with the oppressed, and always against the oppressor . . . I am a non-resistant and I not only desire, but have labored unremittingly to effect, the peaceful abolition of slavery . . . yet, as a peace man—an 'ultra' peace man—I am prepared to say, 'Success to every slave insurrection at the South.'"[54] Whenever a government stood for despotism and tyranny, as the antebellum political order did in Garrison's thinking, "treason" became "a sublime duty."[55] The South's own treason, however, required Garrison to recast his disunion position, leading to the radical son's return to the constitutional fold. After 1860, Garrison vigorously defended "the right and duty of the Government, under the Constitution, to exert all its power to suppress" the traitors.[56]

53. Ibid., 445.

54. Garrison, *Documents of Upheaval*, 266–67.

55. Garrison, "To George Thompson," in *Letters of William Lloyd Garrison, Volume V*, 72.

56. Ibid., 70.

This was not inconsistent with his earlier calls for disunion and "success to . . . insurrection," he insisted through a coherent but convoluted chain of logic; for the South's rebellion, in defiance of the legal system that was structurally biased in its own favor, meant that the South could now be judged according to its own long-professed values of constitutionalism. As "bad as the Constitution is, it has at last become so intolerable to the Southern slave-traffickers that they will no longer live under it."[57] Because the South had declared "eternal hostility to the Union, common sense dictates that the government is . . . to be favorably regarded by the friends of freedom on that account." The enemy of my enemy is my friend. Conservatives and racists drew inevitable (and not entirely implausible) comparisons between the abolitionists and the Southern secessionists, but the two were diametrically opposed. Disunion had been a repudiation of compromise with injustice and a nonviolent attempt to create a more equal constitutional order without war; secession was a violent power grab by an aristocratic elite willing to trample its own laws to perpetuate its' oppressive self-interests.[58] The government was therefore fully justified in waging war against the South, although it remained the duty of the abolitionist "remnant" to embrace nonviolence as their peculiar social witness, viewing the war as God's punishment on slavery but also on *the North* for having failed to pursue the ways of justice and liberty when it had the chance.

Conclusions

Sharing civic space with persons who hold different conceptions of justice, Mark Graber has argued in *Dred Scott and the Problem of Constitutional Evil*, may often require conscientious citizens to give their "allegiance to a constitutional text and tradition saturated with concessions to evil."[59] Constitutions are not designed to "superimpose a vision of justice on a politics of interest," Graber suggests, but to "foster the conditions necessary for constructive dialogues about the good society."[60] Those who insist upon justice as an overriding constitutional concern therefore do grave

---

57. Ibid., 74.
58. Mayer, *All On Fire*, 522.
59. Graber, *Dred Scott and the Problem of Constitutional Evil*, 1.
60. Ibid., 249–50.

injustice to the ethics of constitutionalism itself, which aims to prevent "the politics of justice from destabilizing political regimes." During the 1860 election, Graber concludes, it was John Bell, not Abraham Lincoln, who demonstrated the clearest understanding of the Constitution by campaigning for the presidency on a single platform: to preserve the Union by upholding bisectional relationships and enforcing the laws of the land. Lincoln's insistence that the controversy over slavery be settled justly and in harmony with majoritarian principles misconstrued the Constitution's historical development and did violence to its meaning, leading the nation down a destructive, risky, and unnecessary path of actual violence. Bell's commitment to pragmatic compromise and ongoing "constitutional conversations" with the South, by contrast, "over time *might* have realized a more just society" and avoided the painful path of war.[61]

While Graber's defense of the legal plausibility of *Dred Scott* and critique of Lincoln's aspirational reading of the Constitution is compelling on many levels, his normative vision of "good" constitutionalism as a form of pragmatic negotiation among political elites acting within established institutions and for the sake of social stability nevertheless fails to provide satisfying answers to some of the most pressing dilemmas for constitutional theory posed by the history of slavery. When, if ever, do goals of justice and human rights outweigh such pragmatic objectives as "the military and economic benefits of national union"?[62] How does one affect political change in a society in which "evil" is so deeply entrenched within a constitutional text or structures of political power that to devote oneself to an ongoing "constitutional conversation" would be tantamount to devoting oneself to the preservation of a highly oppressive status quo, possibly in perpetuity? Was slavery a less compelling reason for constitutional revolution in the 1840s than "taxation without representation" in 1776? Graber's constitutionalism cannot answer these and related questions for obvious reasons. If good constitutionalists are those who, by definition and necessity, read the text in ways that do not fundamentally "destabilize political regimes," good constitutional theory will also have little to say about more radical brands of dissent. Constitutions, as founding texts, do not make provisions for principled rebellion against

---

61. Ibid., 253.
62. Ibid., 248.

themselves, and neither should constitutional scholars. A constitutionalism divided against itself cannot stand.

Garrison's politics of disunion are in many ways the antithesis of Graber's pragmatic constitutionalism. Yet Garrison offers a compelling response to the problem of constitutional evil that is fully consistent with Graber's assertion that peace "is intrinsically more just than war" and that "just causes are better realized by persuasion than by force."[63] It is impossible to say what would actually have happened if the North had seceded from the South as Garrison urged. Instead of collapsing from within as he predicted, an unfettered South might well have pursued an aggressive imperialist policy in Mexico and the Caribbean, leading to an even deeper entrenchment of slavery. Even if the South hadn't pursued an expansionist policy, would its economic and geographical isolation have led, as a matter of "necessity," to its collapse? Economic sanctions, as Garrison appears to have desired, contributed to the peaceful unraveling of apartheid South Africa, which has undoubtedly experienced greater social and political stability than it would have had independence been achieved through a bloody civil war. Yet sanctions have so far failed to topple an oppressive and entrenched regime in Burma. Further, in the antebellum South, unlike in contemporary Burma, oppression was rabidly supported by a majority of the population. The historical and comparative evidence therefore offers no clear reply, one way or the other, to the Garrisonian counterfactual. It is clear, though, that the Civil War *did* poison the Union with a legacy of hatred, bitterness, and tension, just as Garrison predicted, scarring the nation in ways that continue to be felt up to the present day. Disunion, accompanied by an aggressive policy of containment, *might* in the long run have ended slavery without war and without the persistent deformations of legalized racism sanctioned for another hundred years under a still conservative and largely unreconstructed Constitution designed to protect Southern states rights.[64]

Whether or not Garrison offered the best solutions to the concrete constitutional and legal dilemmas of pre-Civil War America, his politics highlight the importance of political outsiders and dissenters in the American constitutional experiment. Whether disunion would have prevented or merely delayed and aggravated the Civil War, one thing is clear to this reader: Garrison was not a sinister or unpatriotic malcontent, even

---

63. Ibid., 253.
64. See Les Benedict, "Preserving the Constitution," 65–90.

Anarchy and Apocalypse

in the act of burning the Constitution, but a quintessential American in the revolutionary Yankee mold. "[H]e sought to break the shell of a dead culture to liberate the inner life of conscience, to rend asunder the forms that kept both black and white people in bondage to false sovereigns, and to animate the ethical ideals of the beloved community," Mayer writes.[65] A consistent commitment to peace can only be practically and theoretically linked with a consistent commitment to justice, however, by individuals who recognize constitutions to be relative rather than absolute goods, and who therefore do not hesitate to weigh, and if necessary abandon, oppressive political texts and relationships in the light of what Garrison and his fellow pacifist abolitionists referred to as "higher laws." Garrison's agitation against the Constitution recalled the Protestant reformers and, still further back, the politics of the Hebrew prophets. He also anticipated, and in many ways inspired, the politics of the great moral revolutionaries of the twentieth century. Garrisonian "fanaticism" was a direct influence on Thoreau when he penned his 1849 essay, "Civil Disobedience." Thoreau's essay was a major influence on Gandhi, whose commitment to *satyagraha*, or "truth force," led him to publicly burn his racial identity card in defiance of British law. Gandhi's politics would in turn inspire the politics of Martin Luther King Jr., who said it "is as much a moral obligation to refuse to cooperate with evil as it is to cooperate with good."[66] The fact that most Americans today think of the Constitution as embodying the radical dream of racial equality articulated by King from the steps of the Lincoln Memorial thus illustrates the disturbing yet vibrant influence of religious dissenters, and of Garrison's prophetic imagination in particular, in American legal and political history.

—2007

---

65. Mayer, *All On Fire*, 445.
66. King, "Love, Law, and Civil Disobedience," in *A Testament of Hope*, 48.

8 · *Language in Defense of the Indefensible*

Lessons from the Village of Ben Suc

The mendacity and criminality of America's war in Vietnam are matters of historical record, yet easily forgotten is the role that "objective," "balanced," and "responsible" language played to defend the indefensible. In the article that follows I will examine the relationship between language and violence through a close reading of the U.S. Army's history of its attack on the village of Ben Suc, *Cedar Falls-Junction City: A Turning Point*, by Lieutenant General Bernard Rogers. With today's new Washington planners attempting to disburse billions of dollars in development and reconstruction aid in Iraq in the midst of a heated insurgency war, the village of Ben Suc serves as a prescient reminder from history of what "aid," "development," and "humanitarianism" can mean in the context of an ongoing foreign invasion. Ben Suc also points toward an unsettling kinship between debased language, social sciences, and pathologies of technocratic control. My argument is an essentially linguistic one: to understand the nature of violence in our age, we must learn to pay attention to words.

I

The use of technocratic double-speak as a mask for violence is perhaps nowhere more incisively analyzed than in George Orwell's essay, "Politics and the English Language." "Defenseless villages are bombarded from the air, the inhabitants driven out into the countryside, the cattle machine-gunned, the huts set on fire with incendiary bullets: this is called *pacification*," Orwell wrote in 1946. "Millions of peasants are robbed of

Anarchy and Apocalypse

their farms and sent trudging along the roads with no more than they can carry: this is called *rectification of frontiers* . . . Such phraseology is needed if one wants to name things without calling up mental pictures of them."[1] Orwell identified four ways that truth is shrouded in cocoons of debased speech by the perpetrators of deadly political action: pretentious diction; verbal false limbs; dying metaphors; and meaningless vocabulary. The U.S. Army's official account of its assault on the village of Ben Suc, *Cedar Falls-Junction City: A Turning Point*, offers a classic case study in all four.

In May of 1966, General Westmoreland ordered Operation Cedar Falls. Cedar Falls was to be a strike at what the military called the "Iron Triangle," stretching from Ben Suc to Ben Cat to Phu Guong in South Vietnam. The area was "a haven" for communists and so "a dagger pointed at Saigon." The Americans were determined to put an end to communist activity in the area by "rupturing and neutralizing the control structure" and destroying "hostile infrastructure."[2] Yet the "control structure" of Ben Suc—whose people willingly supported the Vietnamese insurgency—was the village of Ben Suc itself. Hence, "The objective area was to be . . . cleared of all civilians, stripped of concealment, and declared a specified strike zone."[3] "In conjunction with the other services, the Army has fought in support of a national policy of assisting an emerging nation to develop governmental processes of its own choosing, free of outside coercion," Major General Verne Bowers explained.[4] Ben Suc, however, had failed to resist the "outside coercion" of the Vietnamese communists, so the villagers were now to be "evacuated" by American forces to "relocation camps" constructed by USAID. After the villagers were gone, Ben Suc would be razed to the ground.

Early on the morning of January 8, 1967, sixty helicopters unloaded approximately five hundred U.S. soldiers in and around Ben Suc. The soldiers began to herd the population, taken by total surprise, toward the village center. Helicopters with loud speakers meanwhile flew overhead, instructing the people to gather at an old schoolhouse. There was no armed resistance, though some sniper fire was reported and several

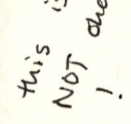

---

1. Orwell, "Politics and the English Language," in *Inside the Whale*, 153.
2. Rogers, *Cedar Falls-Junction City*, 16, 27.
3. Ibid., 19.
4. Ibid., iii.

Language in Defense of the Indefensible

soldiers injured themselves when they wandered into a minefield. "[T]hose who attempted to evade and leave the village were engaged by the blocking forces ... By 1030, 8 January, Ben Suc was securely in the hands of the friendly forces."[5] The Americans quickly set up tents to dispense food and medical aid to the villagers. "Since the inhabitants of Ben Suc had not received medical assistance for three years and were in only fair health, South Vietnamese and U.S. medical teams examined them and provided medical and dental care as they awaited interrogation."[6]

After spending the night under American guard, nearly six thousand villagers from Ben Suc and outlying areas were loaded onto trucks, boats, and helicopters and were taken to relocation camps at Phu Cuong and Phu Loi. Here, "Thanks to the immediate assistance of a task force from the Big Red One under Major Carl R. Grantham, latrines were dug, wood and water were made available, a buffalo wallow was dug and filled with water, a cattle enclosure was built, dozens of Arctic tents were pitched, and hardships were eased for the displaced families."[7] The "hardships" had been compounded by "security measures taken during the planning phase," but the "systematic evacuation" was performed "as humanely as possible." The Army account praises Major Generals DePuy and Hay for their "intricate planning, rapid and decisive execution of actions, and employment of new concepts, coupled with the bravery and skill of our troops" which "made these two operations the success they were."[8] Cedar Falls and Junction City were "the first multidivisional operations in Vietnam to be conducted according to a preconceived plan," and they proved that large-scale operations "do have a place in counterinsurgency warfare today."[9]

The author of *Cedar Falls-Junction City: A Turning Point* was himself an eyewitness to the event. Lieutenant General Bernard Rogers, a Rhodes scholar who studied economics at Oxford University, was asked to write the official Army history by General Westmoreland. The work was completed in 1973, six years after the operation and presumably with full access to all the relevant military documents.

5. Ibid., 43.
6. Ibid., 38.
7. Ibid., 34, 40.
8. Ibid., vi.
9. Ibid., v.

II

There are several things we may note about Rogers's writing. First, it is filled with pretentious abstractions and meaningless phrases that convey an air of scientific objectivity where none exists. Consider the boast that Cedar Falls and Junction City were "the first multidivisional operations in Vietnam to be conducted according to a preconceived plan." Eliminating the redundant word *preconceived* reveals that this was the military's first combined operation conducted *according to a plan*. More disturbing forms of verbal subterfuge follow. "Necessitating this increasing commitment of U.S. forces and resources to South Vietnam was the concomitant growth in the size and quality of the Viet Cong and North Vietnamese cadres in the south," Rogers writes.[10] What he means but cannot say is: *The communists were winning so we had to send more men.* "Some small arms fire was received but was quickly suppressed" we read—and with effort can decipher: *People shot at us but we killed them or scared them away.*[11] Meanwhile, "those who attempted to evade and leave the village were engaged by the blocking forces." Engaged? Blocking? It seems that *Villagers who tried to flee were assaulted by the attacking forces.*

When language is being used to hide the truth, Orwell pointed out, pretentious, hyphenated, and Latinized words choke the page, "like tea leaves blocking a sink."[12] Thus: "Operation Attleboro introduced the large-scale, multi-organization operation to the war [and] proved that, within a matter of hours, well-trained and professionally led organizations with proper logistic support could deploy large numbers of battalions to an active operational area."[13] The war "required superimposing the immensely sophisticated tasks of a modern army upon an underdeveloped environment and adapting them to demands covering a wide spectrum."[14] And so forth. What is not truism is gibberish.

Much of *Operation Cedar Falls-Junction City* is written in either the passive voice or with slovenly verbal phrases rather than with simple verbs. Often we cannot determine who is acting or upon whom. "By the spring of 1963 President Ngo Dinh Diem was being accused of provok-

10. Ibid., 2.
11. Ibid., 37.
12. Orwell, "Politics and the English Language," 151.
13. Rogers, *Cedar Falls-Junction City*, 12.
14. Ibid., iii.

ing an adverse reaction among the people. Especially were the Buddhists unhappy."[15] Who was accusing Diem? The Buddhists? The people? Or were the Buddhists the ones being *provoked*? It is impossible to say. "Finally, on 1 November 1963, Diem was overthrown and assassinated. There followed a period of political instability which featured many coups and countercoups."[16] But who killed Diem? The people? Unhappy Buddhists? The Viet Cong? Propriety does not permit Rogers to write that Diem was murdered by his own Vietnamese generals after their Washington controllers gave them the green light. But there is no need to lie when passive verbal constructions will do. Therefore, "It was then [in the late spring of 1965] that U.S. ground forces were requested and, starting in July, began to arrive in substantial numbers. By August 1965 U.S. forces were being committed to combat."[17] Who requested the ground forces? Who committed them to combat? We are never told, nor does the text leave many clues. The fact that additional American soldiers were requested by the American government itself is not a matter the historian wishes us to meditate deeply upon.

Where Rogers tries to enliven his prose, he invariably resorts to stale metaphors and clichés. The "airborne-waterborne, one-two punch made the Saigon River a boundary they could not afford to come near"; "the regiment knifed toward its objectives"; the "Iron Triangle" was "a dagger pointed at Saigon"; the army began to "hammer the enemy against the anvil"; "Hurting from the whipping it had taken, the [Viet Cong] 9th Division once again disappeared into its sanctuaries to lick its wounds," etc.[18] "Orthodoxy," Orwell observed, "of whatever colour, seems to demand a lifeless, imitative style."[19] This can take the form not only of dying metaphors and clichés, but of ideological stock phrases. *Peoples of the free world, challenges ahead, struggle for democracy, imperialist aggression, class conflict, bourgeois interests, neoliberal order*—one can hardly speak about politics without resorting to such vagaries. The words communicate no clear meaning, but people continue to exchange them knowingly, like secret handshakes at a fraternity initiation rite. Such euphonious

---

15. Ibid., 3.
16. Ibid., 3–4.
17. Ibid., 5.
18. Ibid., 12, 15, 17, 44, 52.
19. Orwell, "Politics and the English Language," 152.

Anarchy and Apocalypse

sounds, Orwell suggested, are primarily noises to "anesthetize a portion of one's brain." "A speaker who uses that kind of phraseology has gone some distance towards turning himself into a machine."[20]

The moral void we detect at the heart of Rogers's history therefore stems from an essentially linguistic betrayal. This betrayal of honest speech leads Rogers to an even more fatal cognitive failure: a failure of imagination. His detached and pseudo-scientific vocabulary does not permit him to enter imaginatively into the lives of the people of Ben Suc. So he discerns no ethical or logical contradiction between the Army's destruction of the village on the one hand and its "humanitarian" provision of food and medicine to the "evacuees" on the other. The two actions are simply two sides of the same managerial goal: power and control. He writes that "hardships were eased for the displaced families," and on the same page: "All that remained for the 1st Division troops was the razing of Ben Suc after its inhabitants had been removed. As the villagers and their belongings moved out, bulldozers, tankdozers, and demolition teams moved in."[21] On occasion, Rogers *does* feel tinges of unease. The sight of the "natives of Ben Suc . . . waiting to be transported to the temporary camp" was "pathetic and pitiful." But a rush of stock phrases quickly fills the interpretive gap. Difficulties "faced during the evacuation" were "relatively few and small in comparison with those problems facing the members of the U.S. Office of Civil Operations who were charged with assisting the South Vietnamese in preparing and operating the relocation center." In fact, *"there were still moments of humor, even for the evacuees"* (my emphasis):

> At one point in the evacuation, a sow became separated from her twelve pigs as they were being loaded on one of the giant Chinook helicopters. She loudly made her loss known. General DePuy, who happened to stop by the loading site and learned of the mishap, instructed: "I want that sow reunited with her pigs before nightfall." Before long, Helper 6 had the sow on her way to the relocation camp.[22]

---

20. Ibid., 152, 155.
21. Rogers, *Cedar Falls-Junction City*, 40.
22. Ibid., 39.

III

In her "report on the banality of evil," *Eichmann in Jerusalem*, Hannah Arendt observed that Adolph Eichmann appeared at his trial less a "monster" than a victim, in some sense, of his own speech. "Officialese is my only language," he apologized to the court. "The longer one listened to him," Arendt writes, "the more obvious it became that his inability to speak was closely connected with an inability to think, namely, to think from the standpoint of somebody else. No communication was possible with him, not because he lied but because he was surrounded by the most reliable of all safeguards against words and the presence of others, and hence against reality as such."[23] It is hardly surprising that political power should corrupt honest speech. What *is* important to observe among the managers of state-sponsored violence is the necessity of a peculiarly dissembling and technocratic language, not only to deceive others but also to deceive themselves.

It is also vital to see the technocratic dialects of policy-makers in terms of processes of indoctrination and thought control in liberal societies. One cannot mouth—or passively accept—a phrase like "hostile infrastructure" to describe a civilian village without having first achieved a high level of education. The tricks of language-masking contained in Rogers's mendacious history of Ben Suc are in fact the essential ingredients of respectable scholarship. They may be found in almost every academic article, in every leading journal, across all academic disciplines. In particular, Noam Chomsky observed in his 1967 essay, "The Responsibility of Intellectuals," they tend to proliferate in the social and behavioral sciences, where linguistic posturing allows "experts" "to imitate the surface features of sciences that really have significant intellectual content."[24] An article from the journal *World Development*, pulled almost at random, illustrates:

> Technological change leads to access to crops that are high in nutrients and empowers the poor by increasing their access to decision-making processes, increasing their capacity for collective action, and reducing their vulnerability to shocks, through asset accumulation ... Literate farmers are more able to assimilate

---

23. Arendt, "Banality and Conscience," in *The Portable Hannah Arendt*, 324.

24. Chomsky, "Responsibility of Intellectuals," in *American Power and the New Mandarins*, 339.

information and make effective use of the new technologies that become available.[25]

To some extent, the obtuseness of the quote (which is in fact remarkably clear by normal academic standards) might be the regrettable but unavoidable price of its precision; "vulnerability to shocks" and "asset accumulation" might convey well-defined ideas to policy-makers that cannot be replaced with simpler English. Still, how much meaning would have been lost had the writer said: "New technology helps farmers to feed themselves and literate farmers are the best learners"? By what unwholesome intellectual paths does *learning* become "assimilating information"? The political correctness of the article and its author are not in question. But why is it, we must ask, that the linguistic conventions of otherwise responsible scholarship in the social and policy sciences foster, and in fact demand, a grammar not far removed from the language of the Washington architects of the Vietnam war?

For Chomsky, the answer has much to do with relations of power, and particularly the privileged role of intellectual specialists in modern societies. There are legitimate things to be learned and explored within the social sciences, Chomsky allows, but he insists that the idea of an "expert" in social theory is almost entirely self-serving and fraudulent. The "Welfare State technician finds justification for his special and prominent social status in his 'science', specifically, in the claim that social science can support a technology of social tinkering on a domestic or international scale." The academic-turned-policy-consultant "argues that the special conditions on which his claim to power and authority are based are, in fact, the only general conditions by which modern society can be saved."[26] Hence the need for an abstract, technical-sounding vocabulary—not to make the facts more clear, but to make them *less* decipherable to the uninitiated while at the same time inducing conformity among the neophytes. Hence also the need to suppress those humanistic categories of speaking and writing—forthrightness, indignation—by which the veneer of "objectivity" might be punctured—even when the specialists themselves reject the idea of *objectivity* in principle. Yet for those genuinely concerned with "moral issues and human rights, or over the traditional problems of

---

25. Thirtle et al., "Impact of Research-Led Agricultural Productivity Growth," 1965–66.

26. Chomsky, "Responsibility of Intellectuals," 345.

man and society," Chomsky maintains, "'social and behavioral science' has nothing to offer beyond trivialities."[27]

Chomsky's indictment of the social sciences may be overdrawn, but his analysis of the political uses of technocratic speech should not be hastily dismissed. "The great enemy of clear language is insincerity," Orwell wrote. "Where there is a gap between one's real and one's declared aims, one turns as it were instinctively to long words and exhausted idioms, like a cuttlefish squirting out ink . . . But if thought corrupts language, language can also corrupt thought. A bad usage can spread by tradition and imitation, even among people who should and do know better."[28] The extent to which the U.S. Army's rendition of what happened in Ben Suc reads as a sober history reveals the extent to which our own speech habits rest upon insincerity—upon decadent and finally treacherous modes of communication. These ways of thinking and talking, inculcated primarily through institutions of formal learning, are what allow sane and reasonable people to condone acts of unimaginable savagery with perfect equanimity.

IV

Since Wittgenstein, Foucault, and Derrida, the idea that words are merely vacuous effusions of power relations—that there is no "truth," only "discourse"—has become something of an academic commonplace. I do not stand in this line of thought. It seems to me that any coherent critique (as opposed to sheer deconstruction) of language must finally rest upon what George Steiner describes as a wager in "substantiation," an assumption of the "necessary possibility" that language can convey real meaning.[29] To say that there is debased speech is to imply that there is such a thing as truthful speech as well.

The claim cannot, of course, be proven, but it can be illustrated. Jonathan Schell, a reporter for *The New Yorker* who accompanied "Charlie" Company into the village of Ben Suc, describes the same events as Lieutenant General Rogers. But his report, "The Village of Ben Suc," stands in relationship to Roger's history as a photograph to its negative.

27. Ibid., 339.
28. Orwell, "Politics and the English Langauge," 154.
29. Steiner, *Real Presences*, 3–4.

Anarchy and Apocalypse

Schell's prose is personal, journalistic, concrete, and imaginative—all of the things social science and policy stylists strive to avoid. Yet for precisely these reasons, it shines a truthful light on Ben Suc where Rogers's "objective" style casts only disorienting shadows.

Schell's ability to imaginatively empathize with the lives of the people of Ben Suc is clear from first lines of his article, in which he describes the village prior to the American attack. The details he selects, inadmissible within most frameworks of "responsible" policy analysis and debate, reveal what the detached words *target*, *secret base*, and *fortified supply center* actually mean—and what bomb navigators and strategic planners cannot afford to think long about if they are to sanely keep their jobs.

Before 1967, Ben Suc was a village of some thirty-five hundred people inside "a small loop of the slowly meandering Saigon River," about thirty miles from Saigon. Most of the villagers of Ben Suc were rice-farmers "engaged in tilling the exceptionally fertile paddies bordering the river and in tending the extensive orchards of mangos, jackfruit, and an unusual strain of large grapefruit."[30] Some were merchants of Chinese ancestry who ran restaurants and hair shops or sold medicines, herbs, bicycles, and other items in the village center. Ben Suc had no electricity and few machine tools. Labor was done by hand and with teams of water buffalo. It was, however, a prosperous village that sold rice and vegetables to neighboring areas. "Some of the marriages in the village were arranged and some were love matches. Although parents—particularly the girls' parents—didn't like it, couples often sneaked off in the evenings for secret rendezvous in the tall bamboo groves or in glades of banana trees."[31] Most of the people of Ben Suc were Buddhists. Some were Confucians. Politically, almost all were communists. They voluntarily supported the National Liberation Font (NLF)—which had routed government troops in the area in 1964 and which the Americans called the "Viet Cong"—by paying taxes of up to 10 percent of their harvests, carrying supplies for NLF troops, staffing a hidden hospital in the jungle, building blockades across roads and teaching their children not only reading, writing, and multiplication tables but also revolutionary slogans.[32]

---

30. Schell, "Village of Ben Suc," in *The Real War*, 59.
31. Ibid., 61.
32. Ibid., 64–66.

Language in Defense of the Indefensible

When the Americans attacked, Rogers writes, "those who attempted to evade and leave the village were engaged by the blocking forces."[33] Concretely, this is what Schell witnessed:

> A Vietnamese man on a bicycle appeared, pedaling rapidly along the road from the direction of the village . . . he had, it appeared, already run a long gauntlet of American soldiers without being stopped. But when he had ridden about twenty yards past the point where he first came in sight, there was a burst of machine-gun fire from a copse thirty yards in front of him . . . he was hurled off his bicycle into a ditch . . . The man with the Minolta camera, who had done the firing from the vegetable patch, stood up after about a minute and walked over to the ditch, followed by one of the engineers. The Vietnamese in the ditch appeared to be about twenty, and he lay on his side without moving, blood flowing from his face . . . The engineer leaned down, felt the man's wrist and said, "He's dead." . . . Then the engineer said, with a tone of finality, "That's a V.C. for you. He's a V.C., all right. That's what they wear. He was leaving town. He had to have some reason."[34]

We now have a clear picture of what Rogers means when he writes: "the enemy was unable to offer any cohesive resistance."[35] We also have good reason to fear what is actually contained in the sentence: "During the two and one-half hours since the initial landing, a total of forty enemy had been killed in action."[36] The logic is inescapable. *They tried to escape so they must have been Viet Cong. They were Viet Cong so we killed them. They must have been Viet Cong because now they're dead.* "The term 'hostile civilians,'" Schell notes, "was a new one, invented during Operation Cedar Falls for the people in the villages that had been marked for destruction. The question of what to call these villagers was one of many semantic problems that the Army had to solve."[37]

Another was what to call the villagers after they had been "relocated" under the "New Life Hamlet program." "At the scene of the evacuation, [the Army] usually used the phrase 'hostile civilians,' which hinted that all the villagers at least supported the enemy . . . But later, at Phu Loi,

---

33. Rogers, *Cedar Falls-Junction City*, 37.
34. Schell, "Village of Ben Suc," 91–92.
35. Rogers, *Cedar Falls-Junction City*, 37.
36. Ibid., 37.
37. Schell, "Village of Ben Suc," 127.

Anarchy and Apocalypse

the officials in charge reverted to the more familiar term 'refugees,' which suggested that the villagers were not themselves the enemy but were 'the people,' fleeing the enemy."[38] This sliding vocabulary to describe the villagers of Ben Suc, without any regard for essential meanings, fits well with Derrida's structuralism. ["Human," we have been told, is a logocentric Occidental construct, not an essence but the "site" of linguistic play. But in Ben Suc, such play helped to sustain a deadly verbal game among soldiers and policy-makers alike.] "This is wonderful!" Colonel White exclaimed to two USAID workers after the villagers had been herded into the camp, surrounded by barbed wire, their homes already bulldozed and (for extra measure) bombed behind them. "I've never seen anything like it. It's the best civilian project I've ever seen . . . We've got shelter up for almost a thousand people here in one day."[39]

And yet. A single encounter in Schell's report reveals all. "You see, they do have some—well, methods and practices we are not accustomed to, that we wouldn't use if we were doing it," Captain Shipman explained to Schell after Schell stumbled upon a tent in the "relocation camp" where South Vietnamese intelligence officers were torturing a man believed to be Viet Cong:

> But the thing you've got to understand is that this is an Asian country, and their first impulse is force . . . Only the fear of force gets results. It's the Asian mind. It's completely different from what we know as the Western mind, and it's hard for us to understand. Look—they're a thousand years behind us in this place, and we're trying to educate them up to our level. We can't just do everything for them ourselves . . . Of course, we believe that that's not the best way to operate, so we try to introduce some changes, but it's very slow . . . I'm only an advisor, and I've made suggestions until I'm blue in the face! Actually, though, we've seen some improvement over the last year. This is a lot better than we used to have.[40]

V

Among the classified U.S. government documents leaked to the press by Daniel Ellsberg in 1971 now known as the *Pentagon Papers,* we find a

38. Ibid., 127.
39. Ibid., 145.
40. Ibid., 112–13.

Language in Defense of the Indefensible

study presented to President Kennedy on May 8, 1961, under the title: "A Program of Action for South Vietnam." The authors of the paper—a task force of specialists from the White House, State Department, Defense Department, Central Intelligence Agency, International Cooperation Administration and United States Information Agency—urge the administration to pursue several long-term "economic" and "development" goals in Indochina. Strangely, these objectives appear not under the heading "Economic" but under the title "Psychological." The government should "Develop agricultural pilot-projects throughout the country with a view toward exploiting their beneficial psychological effects." Such enterprises, the planners write, "would be accomplished by combined teams of Vietnamese Civic Action personnel, Americans in the Peace Corps, Filipinos in Operation Brotherhood, and other Free World nationals."[41] Only in a special annex to the report, under the title "Covert Actions," do we learn of other actions to be undertaken alongside the above: "C. Unconventional Warfare: . . . In Laos, infiltrate teams under light civilian cover to Southeast Laos to locate and attack Vietnamese Communist bases . . . In North Vietnam . . . conduct Ranger raids and similar military actions . . . increase gray broadcasts . . . Support covertly the GVN . . . to counteract tendencies toward a 'political solution.'"[42]

The war in Vietnam, "A Program of Action for South Vietnam" reveals, was conceived by its architects from an early stage as being critically linked to "development," with "economic projects" explicitly "designed to accompany the counter-insurgency effort" in a complementary and parallel fashion. There was no contradiction in the minds of the Washington planners between gray broadcasts, Ranger raids, and napalm bombing on the one hand, and the construction of hospitals, schools, and agricultural pilot-projects on the other. Both were essential means to the same end: victory over the communists and integration of Vietnam into the American sphere of influence and control. At the same time, the architects of the war found it necessary to distinguish between humanitarianism and violence, both to themselves and before the public. Development is referred to in the *Pentagon Papers* as "the other half," or "winning hearts and minds"—euphemistic phrases that suggest both a clear division of labor as well as a sense moral clarity. Development was in some sense

---

41. *Pentagon Papers*, 127.
42. Ibid., 129.

Anarchy and Apocalypse

related to the war—it was its other *half*—yet it was also fundamentally different from it—it was its *other* half. In a small, rice-farming village located in a meandering loop of the Saigon River in 1967, these distinctions were bulldozed to shambles.

The lessons of Ben Suc have not been learned by today's new Washington planners, who speak again about "winning hearts and minds," "humanitarianism" and "development" as the "other half" of the insurgency war in Iraq. Or, it may be, the lessons *have* been learned all too well. History offers little hope that "aid" and "development" will not continue to be corrupted by their proximity to coercive power. It is left to honest women and men to find the language necessary for resistance.

—2004

9 · Obama's Niebuhrian Moment

In his December 10, 2009, Nobel Peace Prize acceptance speech, President Obama offered a vigorous defense of the just war tradition in response to problems of evil and injustice in the world. More than this, however, he offered a moral vision that closely followed, without any direct reference, the ideas of perhaps the most influential American theologian of the twentieth century. In a much cited 2007 *New York Times* article, David Brooks wrote that he asked then-Senator Obama as an off-the-cuff question if he had ever read Reinhold Niebuhr. "I love him," Obama replied. "He's one of my favorite philosophers." He then proceeded, Brooks reported, to discuss the theologian's ideas with great enthusiasm and incision.[1] In fact, Obama's speech in Oslo can be read as a concise restatement of Niebuhr's political ethics as a guide to U.S. foreign policy for the twenty-first century.

Niebuhr was born in 1892 in Wright City, Missouri, into the home of a German Evangelical Synod minister. He decided to follow in his father's footsteps and attended Yale Divinity School before entering a working-class parish in Detroit, where he served as a pastor for thirteen years until 1928. During this period, he was a committed socialist and pacifist in the "social gospel" tradition, serving as a community organizer alongside union leaders in the fight to improve labor conditions in Henry Ford's factories. At the outbreak of World War II, however, Niebuhr's politics underwent a radical change. Breaking decisively with Christians who continued to urge nonviolence as the only path to peace, Niebuhr (who was by then Professor of Practical Theology at Union Theological Seminary in New York) rejected pacifism as morally insipid and politi-

---

1. Brooks, "Obama, Gospel and Verse." Online: http://select.nytimes.com/2007/04/26/opinion/26brooks.html.

Anarchy and Apocalypse

cally irresponsible in the face of Nazi evil. Instead, he urged a form of political engagement that he described as "Christian Realism."

Niebuhr's Christian Realism, which has been the dominant political theology of America's liberal establishment since the 1940s, rests upon a set of seemingly self-evident claims about the "tragic" dimensions of human nature and history; an assertion of the inescapable burden of "necessity" that confronts those who rule; and an appeal to virtues of humility and restraint in the exercise of force for the sake of the common good. For Niebuhr, Christian political thought must be guided by at least four basic truths. These are, it turns out, the same axioms that must guide all wise and responsible statesmen, whether or not they happen to *be* Christians.

Niebuhr's Political Theology Revisited

First, the enlightened policy-maker must maintain a constant awareness of the tragedy and irony of history. According to Andrew Bacevich, Niebuhr's 1952 book *The Irony of American History* is "the most important book ever written on U.S. foreign policy."[2] Its central insight, Bacevich writes, is that Americans must "give up their Messianic dreams" and cease their "vain attempts to remake the world in our own image"[3]; for history, Niebuhr saw, is stubbornly resistant to all efforts to control its outcomes, as well as to all utopian political projects. The tragedy of history is that sometimes choices for evil must be made for the sake of the greater good. The irony of history is that the good can often become evil and strength can often become weakness as a result of hubris and folly.

The irony and tragedy of history, in Niebuhr's thinking, could be traced back to innate aspects of the human condition, which leads to his second critical insight: the sinfulness of man. Niebuhr's liberalism caused him to read Scripture as a wellspring of deep mythological truths about human experience and psychology. Among these mythological insights into anthropological questions was the idea of original sin (which Niebuhr also took from his readings of St. Augustine, Luther, and Calvin). Human depravity or "fallenness" accounted for the persistence of violence and war in the world. Responsible political action thus could not be based upon pious hopes in either eradicating conflict or changing recalcitrant

2. Bacevich, "Introduction" to *Irony of American History*, ix.
3. Ibid., xvi–xvii.

106

human nature (through, for example, programs of education, economic development, or moral reform). Instead, heads of state needed to deal unflinchingly with the facts of self-interest and power in the "real" world. If necessary, they also needed to accept dirty hands out of a sober awareness that all are implicated in the guilt of the human race and that violence is an inescapable part of the fallen human condition.

The third key axiom in Niebuhr's political theory is the need to balance "realism" and "idealism." Although Niebuhr described his political ethics as "realist," like E. H. Carr he also emphasized the dangers of a politics divorced from moral ideals and transcendent values. Sheer realism, he declared, leads to "cynicism." Realism and idealism thus need to be held in constant dialectical tension "lest we become callous to the horror of war" or "forget the ambiguity of our own actions."[4] Christian pacifists naively—and dangerously—failed to see that "the Cross is not an instrument of social policy."[5] Yet by their refusal to participate in acts of violence and war they also helped to remind responsible Christian Realists that, "the true end of man is brotherhood, and that love is the law of life."[6] Warfare is always, at best, a necessary evil.

Finally, Niebuhr drew a sharp distinction between personal morality and the exigencies of statecraft. While he urged a dynamic tension between realism and idealism in international relations, he at the same time insisted that political actors detach their private ethical—and especially religious—commitments from their public decision-making. In a 1951 article in the journal *Christianity and Society*, Niebuhr wrote that, "religion deals with life's ultimate ends and meanings, while politics must inevitably strive for proximate ends of life and must use ambiguous means to attain them." Hence, he declared, "it is dangerous to claim the sanctity of the ultimate for political ends and means."[7] Grace, Niebuhr explained elsewhere, is what frees the Christian "to act in history, to give his devotion to the highest values he knows, to defend those citadels of civilization of which necessity and historic destiny have made him the defender."[8] We may freely participate in morally ambiguous political actions to preserve

4. Niebuhr, "Why the Christian Church is Not Pacifist," 119.
5. As cited in Coffey, *Political Realism in American Thought*, 90.
6. Niebuhr, "Why the Christian Church is Not Pacifist," 119.
7. As cited in Coffey, *Political Realism in American Thought*, 108.
8. Niebuhr, "Why the Christian Church is Not Pacifist," 118.

Anarchy and Apocalypse

the social order because God's providence—by grace—can "bring good out of evil."

"I Face the World as It Is": Obama in Norway

Each of these four major themes in Niebuhr's thinking found powerful resonance in President Obama's Nobel Prize acceptance speech, which has drawn praise from both Republicans and Democrats as a courageous reassertion of American power and moral leadership. What Obama in fact did was reassert as the doctrinal basis of his foreign policy the cherished political theology of the two major parties for most of the past century (following the disastrous Straussian heresy of George Bush the younger).

(1) *The tragedy of history*: The great tragedy of history, Obama declared, is that war is terrible but unavoidable. "We must begin by acknowledging the hard truth that we will not eradicate violent conflict in our lifetimes."[9] There will be times when "the use of force is not only necessary but morally justified." A "nonviolent movement could not have halted Hitler's armies." Further, "global security for more than six decades" has rested upon America's defense of democracy through "the strength of our arms." Hence, "To say that force is sometimes necessary is not a call to cynicism—it is a recognition of history; the imperfections of man and the limits of reason."

(2) *The sinfulness of man*: We must face "the core struggle of human nature," Obama asserted. "We are fallible. We make mistakes, and fall victim to the temptations of pride, and power, and sometimes evil. Even those of us with the best intentions will at times fail to right the wrongs before us." "All responsible nations" must therefore "embrace the role that militaries with a clear mandate can play to keep the peace." At the same time, we must heed John F. Kennedy's words and pursue "a more practical, more attainable peace, based not on a sudden revolution in human nature but on a gradual evolution in human institutions."

(3) *The dialectic of realism and idealism*: The great challenge, Obama said, lies in "reconciling these two seemingly irreconcilable truths—that war is sometimes necessary, and war is at some level an expression of human folly." In facing this paradox, we must reject a "stark choice between

---

9. Obama, "A Just and Lasting Peace." Online: http://nobelprize.org/nobel_prizes/peace/laureates/2009/obama-lecture_en.html.

the narrow pursuit of interests or an endless campaign to impose our values"—the paths of "realism or idealism." What is needed is a course of "enlightened self-interest." The nonviolent tactics of religious leaders such as Gandhi and Martin Luther King Jr. in this regard are not "practical or possible in every circumstance." Yet as exemplars of the "law of love," their visions can still "be the North Star that guides us on our journey."

(4) *The separation of personal morality from the duties of public life*: At a personal level, Obama noted, "I am living testimony to the moral force of non-violence" through King's legacy. "But as a head of state sworn to protect and defend my nation, I cannot be guided by their examples alone. I face the world as it is, and cannot stand idle in the face of threats to the American people."

Playing Hardball: The Irony of "Christian Realism"

The great irony of Niebuhr's Christian Realism, however, is that in many ways it was not realistic enough, both about itself and about the nature of American power in the post–World War II era. Niebuhr's positions on political questions ranging from the creation of NATO to the doctrine of containment to the Korean War to nuclear armament (all of which he supported) are no more clearly "religious" or "Christian" than those of his friends George Kennan and Hans Morgenthau—fellow political realists who saw no reason to attach religious adjectives to their political philosophy. Of course, this follows directly from Niebuhr's separation of personal morality and religious faith from the sphere of political ethics. But why, then, did Niebuhr describe his politics as *Christian* Realism? What did Christ or the church or the New Testament have to do with it?

The answer is, nothing at all. The "realities" to which Niebuhrian Christian Realism appeals, John Milbank writes, are in fact the "realities" of ancient Stoicism—"not the realities of history, nor the realities of which Christian theology speaks, but simply things generated by its own assumptions, its own language and rhetoric."[10] Niebuhr's use of words like "sin" and "grace" touched deep Calvinist chords in the self-understandings of many Americans and gave his pronouncements on foreign policy an orthodox-sounding varnish. But what Niebuhr provided America's political elites from the 1940s on—and the Truman and Kennedy admin-

---

10. Milbank, *Word Made Strange*, 233.

istrations in particular—was valuable ideological legitimization for more pragmatic policies in the context of Cold War power rivalries. Kennedy liberals "did not so much use Niebuhr's name as feel indebted to his perspective," Richard Fox writes. "He helped them maintain faith in themselves as political actors in a troubled—what he termed a sinful—world. Stakes were high, enemies were wily, responsibility meant taking risks: Niebuhr taught that moral men had to play hardball."[11]

And play hardball the Kennedy administration did. Humiliated by the failed invasion of Cuba at the Bay of Pigs, the President ordered a secret campaign of psychological warfare, sabotage, and attempted assassinations of Castro under the codename "Operation Mongoose." These covert activities helped to generate the Cuban Missile Crisis (considered by many to be Kennedy's "finest hour") in which the United States risked nuclear holocaust for the sake of American "prestige." Defense Secretary Robert McNamara informed Kennedy that the missiles in Cuba did not significantly alter the military balance of power since Soviet nuclear submarines were already operating just off of America's shores. And there were possible diplomatic solutions that Kennedy might have tried instead of high-stakes nuclear brinksmanship (such as an offer to remove the U.S.'s already obsolete Jupiter missiles from the Soviet Union's doorstep in Turkey as a quid pro quo for removal of the missiles in Cuba). But Kennedy refused to consider these options since he deemed it cowardice to "blink" while standing at the edge of the abyss.

Elsewhere in Latin America, Kennedy implemented (as part of his "Alliance for Progress") a rapid buildup of military forces and counterinsurgency programs focused not on "hemispheric defense" as in the past, but on a new strategy of ensuring "internal security." In practice, historian Walter LaFeber writes, "this meant that in Central America the military forcefully maintained the status quo for the oligarchs"—that is, the corrupt elites who kept the majority of people in a state of landlessness and virtual indentured servitude, but who served the interests of U.S. corporations such as United Fruit and Standard Oil.[12] Under the tutelage of the United States Agency for International Development and the School of the Americas, Latin American dictators learned "to use gas guns, helicopters, and other anti-riot equipment." It proved "only a short

11. Fox, *Reinhold Niebuhr*, 276.
12. LaFeber, *Inevitable Revolutions*, 153.

step," LaFeber concludes, "to controlling dissent through sophisticated methods of torture."[13]

The "dirty wars" of the 1980s (in which the Reagan administration trained, equipped, and funded right-wing death squads in Nicaragua, Guatemala, and El Salvador as they crushed peasant guerrillas and murdered socially conscious Catholic priests in the name of saving the free world from communism) are therefore a direct legacy of the policies of the Kennedy administration.

In Vietnam, the President meanwhile ordered a massive troop surge, increasing the number of U.S. military "advisors" from 900 under President Eisenhower to 16,000 by the end of 1963. Kennedy may thus be credited with launching the Vietnam War, including authorizing wide-scale bombing, the use of napalm and chemical defoliants, and the "strategic hamlet" program in which thousands of Vietnamese peasants were forced into concentration camps to deprive the Viet Cong of their "social base." He also gave Vietnamese generals a green light for the 1963 coup that resulted in President Ngo Dinh Diem's assassination. Less than three weeks later, Kennedy himself was assassinated.

This analysis of Kennedy's foreign policy is, of course, thoroughly "realist" in the sense of seeing U.S. actions—no different than those of other great powers in history—as flowing from factors of self-interest and a logic of imperialism (combining, as one would expect, "soft" as well as "hard" approaches). Yet while Niebuhr did come to strongly criticize the war in Vietnam on moral as well as pragmatic grounds, this way of reading American history is *not* Niebuhrian. Niebuhr's rejection of the myth of American Exceptionalism notwithstanding, his Christian Realism did not permit any critique of U.S. power that would radically undermine his goal of *serving* that power, which he took to be the only responsible political course available. Niebuhr saw the United States as deeply flawed (we have "made mistakes," as Obama said in Oslo), yet as a still fundamentally benign and noble force in world affairs. "Our" violence, unlike "theirs," was therefore historically necessary and justified in Niebuhr's political and moral calculus in order to maintain "stability" and preserve the "citadels of civilization."

By justifying tactics of violence and coercion in the name of tragic necessity, Reinhold Niebuhr thus ironically fell victim to what theolo-

---

13. Ibid., 153.

gians Stanley Hauerwas and Michael Broadway describe as "a severe cases of ideological blindness."[14] His account of "reality" affirmed in a religious key the prevailing foreign policy wisdom and elite decision-making of the age—invasions, coups, dirty wars, Mutual Assured Destruction and all.

These facts should give admirers of President Obama's Nobel speech—in which he invoked the memory and spirit of Kennedy while defending an intensification of the war in Afghanistan on just war grounds—considerable pause. It is true that American power has changed in important ways since the height of the Cold War, and Afghanistan is not Vietnam. Nevertheless, the underlying dynamics, structures, and goals of U.S. power have not radically changed since the days of Kennedy's Camelot (which the Obama administration clearly sees itself as recreating in important ways).

A realistic view of U.S. foreign policy will observe, for example, that America's economy is driven by military spending, which consumes more than half of the Federal discretionary budget and is roughly equal to the rest of the world's military spending combined. The Pentagon System has continued despite the end of the Cold War because it is deeply woven into the fabric of American life. Preserving a "permanent war economy" is a form of subsidization for key industries. It is a way of maintaining employment and generating profits among vital constituencies. It is a useful tool for politicians to manage and mobilize the population—and for corporations to manage and mobilize politicians. The result is tremendous institutional pressure on leaders to generate or inflate foreign threats and to export violence abroad in the name of "security" at home, since any major disruption of the arms industry would have massive and undesirable political, social, and economic consequences. It should come as no surprise, in this light, that President Obama's proposed defense budget for 2010, excluding the costs of the wars in Iraq and Afghanistan, is $534 billion—an increase of $20 billion from President Bush's last military budget.[15]

And while Obama's repudiation of torture and promise to close Guantanamo Bay are welcome, his stepped-up campaign of unmanned Predator drone strikes in Afghanistan and Pakistan—which according to

14. Hauerwas and Broadway, "Irony of Reinhold Niebuhr," 50.
15. Pemberton and Smith, "Budget Makes No 'Sweeping Shift' in Security Spending Yet." Online: http://www.ips-dc.org/articles/budget_makes_no_sweeping _shift_in_security_spending_yet.

a recent study by the New America Foundation have killed up to 1000 people during the past three years, one-third of them civilians[16]—underscores a grim reality: the old rules are still very much in effect. The seal of American power is death on the wing, and it is the natives in foreign lands who will continue to pay the cost (although Americans too may someday pay high costs for these policies, as they did on 9/11, in the form of what Chalmers Johnson has called "blowback").

Another Realism: Remembering King's Militant Nonviolence

So what might an alternative *realistic* political ethic be, if not Niebuhr's Christian Realism with its pessimistic view of human nature yet hopelessly optimistic belief that policy-makers can somehow manage a politics of violence without corrupting or destroying the ideals they say they are fighting for? The most eloquent voice for a constructive Christian ethic in times of war remains Martin Luther King Jr., whose sermons and speeches—including his 1964 Nobel Peace Prize address—offer not only a substantive politics of hope but also a profoundly relevant prophetic realism. There are three critical lessons King taught us that are especially vital to recall following President Obama's speech in Oslo.

(1) *See without illusions the real nature of power and violence—and empire—in our age*: In his 1967 address at the Riverside Church in New York, "A Time to Break Silence," King directly linked the cause of civil rights to the war in Vietnam.[17] He spoke, he said, from "a tragic recognition of reality" that racism, poverty, and militarism are deeply intertwined, and that the war was "but a symptom of a far deeper malady within the American spirit." "A nation that continues year after year to spend more money on military defense than on programs of social uplift," he warned, "is approaching spiritual death." While it was necessary to see "the ambiguity of the total situation," it was also necessary to face the fact that the United States—while seeking to "maintain social stability for our investment accounts"—had become "the greatest purveyor of violence in the world today." It was building a house "on political myth," shored up "with the power of new violence."

---

16. Bergen and Tiedemann, "Revenge of the Drones." Online: http://counterterrorism.newamerica.net/publications/policy/revenge_of_the_drones#_ftn1.

17. King, *Testament of Hope*, 231–44.

King proceeded to offer an unsparing catalogue of the brutalities being inflicted on the Vietnamese people by their occupiers, and a searing indictment of U.S. policy as a continuation of European colonialism, driven by a fatal mixture of paternalism and greed. America was "adding cynicism to the process of death," King said, by "refusing to give up the privileges and the pleasures that come from the immense profits of overseas investments." Failure to "undergo a radical revolution in values . . . from a 'thing-oriented' society to a 'person-oriented' society" could only lead, he predicted, to future conflicts in other parts of the globe—conflicts that would ultimately result in America joining "the bleached bones and jumbled residue of numerous civilizations" that had ignored "the fierce urgency of now."

(2) *Reorient your primary loyalties and learn how to think "from below"*: King's militant nonviolence was a direct expression of his commitment to living out the political meaning of the Cross as the instrument of "weakness" by which God had ironically overcome the "principalities and powers" of the world and broken down barriers to create peace between former strangers and enemies. What this meant for King was that, "our loyalties must become ecumenical rather than sectional." People of conscience must now be "bound by allegiances and loyalties which are broader and deeper than nationalism and which go beyond our nation's self-defined goals and positions."

Instead of constructing his political ethics from perspectives of national self-interest and fantasies of control over the means of violence ("But what would *you* do if *you* were President Obama?"), King urged his listeners in Riverside to embrace a politics of engagement *from below*. He sought to reorient the moral imaginations of Americans by insisting that we approach questions of conflict and war through the eyes of the Other: the powerless, the suffering, and even the enemy. "We are called to speak for the weak, for the voiceless, for victims of our nation and for those it calls enemy, for no document from human hands can make these humans any less our brothers."

(3) *Hold those in power accountable to their own highest values, and build concrete and pragmatic bridges to peace*: For the commander-in-chief of the world's most powerful military, an ethic of strict nonviolence is clearly not an option. But as Mennonite theologian John Howard Yoder pointed out, honest just war theorists and pacifists will stand united in opposition to virtually every war since the purpose of the just war tradi-

tion as developed by the Catholic Church was never to *justify* war but to place stringent limits on what those in power can do. And the limits are great. President Obama mentioned King's name no less than four times during his Nobel speech (as well as Aung San Suu Kyi's), demonstrating (one hopes) a rare willingness on the part of a statesman to take seriously the power and courage of nonviolent direct political action. Pacifists should now demonstrate equal understanding and respect for the moral seriousness of the just war tradition by holding Obama accountable to the tradition's high ideals: strict immunity for civilians, force only as a defensive measure of last resort, absolute proportionality of means, and striving for the global good—not merely America's self-interests—as the final end.

King urged the peace movement to pursue a course of "wise restraint and calm reasonableness." He called on the Johnson administration to adhere to international rule of law and outlined phased steps for "the long and difficult process of extricating ourselves" from Vietnam (including creating ground conditions for negotiations, ending interference in neighboring countries, setting dates for the removal of troops, granting asylum to political refugees, and providing humanitarian assistance to help rebuild the country). At the same time, King offered strategic guidance to students, clergy, and others not in public office to resist the draft and engage in acts of civil disobedience. There are ways for Christians to work pragmatically, creatively, and realistically to end conflicts, King demonstrated in the process, without forgetting who they are while inside the belly of the Leviathan.

—2010

10 · *Geometries of Force in Homer's* Iliad

Two Readings

At the outbreak of World War II, two French Jewish intellectuals—Simone Weil and Rachel Bespaloff—wrote responses to Europe's unfolding catastrophe in the form of literary essays on Homer's *Iliad*. Their explorations of violence, power, fate, freedom, and the machine of war, as seen through the lens of ancient Greece's founding epic, have themselves achieved the status of classic political and philosophical texts. Weil and Bespaloff's contrasting readings of the *Iliad* were recently published together for the first time by The New York Review. How does each writer re-imagine the poem to make sense of the human condition and the harsh realities of warfare? In the shadow of totalitarianism and genocide, what moral and political resources do they find in Homer? Does either of the two writers offer a more compelling interpretation of Homer's epic? And what might Weil and Bespaloff—and Homer—have to teach us about the geometries of force today? — proof you don't need the sacred texts of the Bible to consider humanity's condition ¨

Far from Hot Baths: Weil's Pacifist Reading of the *Iliad*

Simone Weil's "*L'Iliade*, ou le poème de la force" first appeared in December of 1940 and January of 1941 in the Marseilles journal *Cahiers du Sud*. Weil, described by Albert Camus as "the only great spirit of our time," was a philosopher who graduated with distinction from the École Normale Supérieure in 1931, a committed socialist who worked in a Renault assembly line and volunteered to fight alongside anarcho-syndicalists in Aragon during the Spanish Civil War, and a convert to Christianity who embraced Catholicism after receiving a mystical vision

Geometries of Force in Homer's Iliad

in 1938.¹ Her meditation on the *Iliad* as a revelation of the universal and dehumanizing effects of force—on victors and vanquished alike—is an essentially antiheroic, spiritual, and even pacifist reading that emphasizes Homer's moral neutrality and the insensibility of all wars.

According to Weil, "The true hero, the true subject, the center of the *Iliad* is force."² The cumulative effect of the poem is not to valorize its warriors, Greek or Trojan, she suggests, but to demonstrate how the human spirit is modified, blinded, deformed, and enslaved under the weight of force, even as individuals imagine force is something they can control, possess, or contain. Weil defines force as "that x that turns anybody who is subjected to it into a thing," and declares that force lies not only at the heart of the poem but "at the very center of human history." The great value of the *Iliad* is its bitter yet unsentimental depiction, in myriad ways, of living beings undergoing violent transformations into sheer matter, corpses dragged behind chariots in the dust, as a result of their contact with force.

Even more dramatically, the *Iliad* shows how a free individual caught up in the machinery of war can be transformed "into a stone . . . into a thing while still alive." In the strange interval of time between when a fighter realizes he is doomed and the sword strikes, his soul is already crushed, petrified, reduced to state in which he is incapable of thinking or hoping. Even those suppliants whose lives are somehow spared by their enemies, such as King Priam at the feet of Achilles, must spend the rest of their days recalling the force of death that once hung over their heads. The result is a permanent scarring or deformation of their psyches that produces "a compromise between a man and corpse." To say that a seemingly alive person is a thing is a logical contradiction. "Yet what is impossible in logic becomes true in life, and the contradiction lodged within the soul tears it to shreds."

But force not only destroys and does violence to the weak in Weil's reading of the *Iliad*. "Force is as pitiless to the man who possesses it, or thinks he does, as it is to its victims; the second it crushes, the first it intoxicates." If human beings are driven, as Nietzsche insists, by a sheer will to power, in Weil's politics all merely human wills to power must ultimately be seen as expressions of hopeless delusion, since the appetite

---

1. Camus as cited by Pinachas, "Introduction," in *Simone Weil Reader*, xvii.
2. Weil, "The *Iliad*, or The Poem of Force," in *War and the Iliad*, 3–37.

117

for power is produced by nothing other than the will *of* power at work in history. It is power itself, in other words, that possesses and manipulates men, not the other way around. Even the most clear-sighted warriors are unable to exercise restraint after experiencing victory in battle. Those who have been temporary channels of force imagine "that destiny has given complete license to them." Patroclus presses his advantage to his own destruction at the hands of Hector. Hector then rejects Polydamas' prudent counsel, refusing to allow the Greeks to escape, insisting instead that the Trojans pursue "glory at the ships."

At the precise moment when force bestows success it thus gives birth to an irresistible blindness or hubris in its carriers that invariably spells their destruction. In Homer's universe there is "not a single man who does not at one time or another have to bow his neck to force." Those "who have force on loan from fate count on it too much and are destroyed." Common soldiers, such as Thersites, may be abused and humiliated by their superiors, but Achilles and Agamemnon will also weep tears of humiliation in their turn. Every fighter in the *Iliad* other than Achilles experiences a defeat in battle, and Achilles is nearly destroyed by the river god Scamander. There is a strict moral economy at work in the poem, Weil writes, so that retribution falls with "a geometrical rigor" on strong and weak alike. "The *Iliad* formulated the principle [that those who take up the sword will die by the sword] long before the Gospels, and in almost the same terms: *Ares is just, and kills those who kill.*" "We are only geometricians of matter; the Greeks were, first of all, geometricians in their apprenticeship to virtue."

Homer's strict geometry of force does not lead, however, to a heightened sense of war's ultimate logic or rationality. Just the reverse: it is the most irrational elements of human behavior that come to the fore in war, radically subverting "just war" theories grounded in notions of prudence, proportionality, and restraint. What are required to win battles are not men of planning and strategy—"battles are fought and decided by men deprived of these faculties, men who have undergone a transformation, who have dropped either to the level of inert matter, which is pure passivity, or to the level of blind force, which is pure momentum." A moderate use of force, even if effective, would require a superhuman capacity of restraint, but those who begin down the path of war prove incapable of resisting the temptation to overreach. Hence, "words of reason drop into the void." Force is at first claimed as a means to necessary ends, but the

Geometries of Force in Homer's Iliad

internal logic of war "effaces all conceptions of a purpose or goal, including even its own 'war aims.'" What we witness in the *Iliad* is an inversion of means and ends, with violence ultimately becoming its own end. The death of one's comrades "arouses a spirit of somber emulation, a rivalry in death." You must fight on, the gods command, or you will offend the dead. The first cause of the war, Helen, is forgotten. It is slaughter that necessitates more slaughter.

Closely related themes may be found in Weil's trenchant essay on Marxism, "Analysis of Oppression," written before her essay on the *Iliad* but published posthumously in 1955. "[P]ower-seeking, owing to its essential incapacity to seize hold of its object, rules out all consideration of an end, and finally comes, through an inevitable reversal, to take the place of all ends," she declares. "Human history is simply the history of the servitude which makes men—oppressed and oppressors alike—the plaything of the instruments of domination they themselves have manufactured, and thus reduces living humanity to being the chattel of inanimate chattels."[3]

If power/force in the *Iliad* is essentially dehumanizing and the battlefield profoundly antiheroic as Weil suggests, where might we locate authentically human modes of existence in the poem? What makes life meaningful, if not the quest for power or glory? For Weil, the *Iliad* alludes, by way of negation and contrast, to the possibility—though rarely the actuality—of another kind of world: "the far-away, precarious, touching world of peace, of the family, the world in which each man counts more than anything else to those about him."[4] There are "luminous moments," "moments of grace" in the poem in which we catch glimpses of human beings fully possessed of their own souls and their own freedom rather than simply intoxicated by the blandishments of power or manipulated by capricious gods. These moments involve such emotions as love, loyalty, and pity, and are often rooted in familial or domestic relations. Thetis weeping for her doomed soon Achilles; Achilles mourning the death of his friend Patroclus; Andromache preparing a hot bath for Hector, not knowing that he is already dead—all of these scenes expose the enervating horrors of war in stark relief and remind Homer's listeners/readers that force makes humans less than they ought to be. Yet "Nearly all the

---

3. Weil, "Analysis of Oppression," in *Simone Weil Reader*, 138.
4. Weil, "The *Iliad*, or The Poem of Force," 3–37.

Iliad takes place far from hot baths. Nearly all of human life, then and now, takes place far from hot baths." War in the *Iliad* is symptomatic of the fact that human beings, in the language of another tradition, are radically *fallen*.

While it would be a mistake to read the *Iliad* in didactic or narrowly moralistic terms, the cumulative effect of the epic, in Weil's reading, is therefore deeply ethical if not theological in its implications. Homer makes us feel "with sharp regret what it is that violence has killed and will kill again." The poem is absolutely impartial to Greeks and Trojans alike, so that Homer's "incurable bitterness" at the fate that conspires to drag humans into a state of perpetual conflict reveals a great *tenderness* toward humanity as a whole. "Nothing precious is scorned, whether or not death is its destiny; everyone's happiness is laid bare without dissimulation or disdain; no man is set above or below the condition common to all men; whatever is destroyed is regretted."

In Praise of Hector: Bespaloff on the Virtues of Resistance

Rachel Bespaloff, though less well known than Weil, was also a brilliant philosopher steeped in existentialist and classical literature. The daughter of Zionist theoretician Daniel Pasmanik, she published one of the earliest articles in French on Heidegger's *Being and Time*, as well as acclaimed essays in the 1930s on thinkers such as Kierkegaard, Gabriel Marcel, and André Malraux. Bespaloff began to compose her own study of the *Iliad* in 1939, arriving at many startlingly similar conclusions to Weil without knowledge of the other's work. After being sent a manuscript of Weil's essay by publisher Jean Grenier, and after the fall of Paris in 1940, however, Bespaloff revised her work in answer to Weil's reading, as well as in response to the crisis of totalitarianism. "De L'*Iliade*" was published three years after Weil's essay in New York, where both women had fled as refugees in 1942 and where both would die tragic deaths involving their own wills. Weil, who had long struggled with anorexia, died in 1943 from complications of tuberculosis while refusing in solidarity with her starving compatriots in occupied France to eat adequate amounts of food. In 1949, Bespaloff sealed her kitchen with towels and turned on the gas oven. She left behind a note saying she was "too fatigued to carry on."[5]

5. Benfy, "Introduction," in *War and the Iliad*, i, xvi–xxiii.

Bespaloff's essay on the *Iliad* is divided into a series of character sketches and philosophical reflections under the titles: "Hector," "Thetis and Achilles," "Helen," "The Comedy of the Gods," "Troy and Moscow," and "Poets and Prophets." Like Weil, Bespaloff stresses the strict geometry of fate at work in the poem, which reduces or elevates Greeks and Trojans alike to a level of common, suffering humanity. Between Hector's degradation of the body of Patroclus and Achilles' degradation of the body of Hector "a rigorous parallelism is kept . . . war devours differences and disparities, shows no respect for the unique."[6] Bespaloff also agrees with Weil that we should view force in the Homeric universe largely as something external to the warriors who wield it. Force possesses and intoxicates, and the culmination of exercising force over others is, paradoxically, the moment when the "strong" man's weakness is exposed and his undoing is sealed. "Force revels only in an abuse that is also self-abuse, in an excess that expends its store," Bespaloff writes. "Homer shows us the limits of force in the very apotheosis of the force-hero."

The *Iliad* thus presents a curious dialectic of power/weakness that is at once tragic and deeply ironic. Achilles' cruelty, we find, springs from his actual "powerlessness to achieve omnipotence." His megalomaniacal and self-destructive attraction to violence betrays "the eternal resentment felt by the will to power" confronted by the impossibility of its own "indefinite expansion." For Homer, contra Nietzsche, it is not the weak man who most clearly evinces the quality of resentment, but the strong man who can "bend everything to his will" and who finds that this is still not enough, that there is no correlation between might and happiness, and that the result of power is a pointless but insatiable appetite for more power.

Yet Bespaloff's view of force in the *Iliad* is more complex than Weil's, for while she recognizes its self-destructive, circular, and illusory nature, she also detects its creative beauty, at least within the universe Homer gives us. "[H]e sees warlike emulation as the fountainhead of creative effort, as the spring of individual energy and of the manly virtues in the community." Homer possesses both "a virile love of war and a virile horror of it." Power is "the supreme illusion of life" but it is also its "supreme reality." It is "divine insofar as it represents a superabundance of life that flashes out in the contempt for death . . . it is detestable insofar as it contains a

---

6. Bespaloff, "On the *Iliad*," in *War and the Iliad*, 43–100.

Anarchy and Apocalypse

fatality that transforms it into inertia, a blind drive that is always pushing it on to the very end of its course . . . the obliteration of the very values it engendered." War, pillage, rage—the ways of Achilles—can deliver only "the glitter of empty triumphs and mad enterprises," Bespaloff asserts. Without Achilles and his tribe, humans would have peace. But without Achilles they would also fall into a deep sleep, "frozen with boredom, till the planet itself grew cold."

The *Iliad*, in Bespaloff's reading, is therefore a more morally ambiguous text than in Weil's reading. Where Weil sees force always and only as transforming radiant spirit into dull matter, Bespaloff allows that force might also transform matter into spirit. Being and becoming, nature and existence, matter and spirit, war and peace—in her poetics, are all caught up in the One of life, just as they are on the shield of Achilles. Hence, "To condemn force, or absolve it, would be to condemn, or absolve life itself." "Who is good in the *Iliad*? Who is bad? Such distinctions do not exist; there are only men suffering, warriors fighting, some winning, some losing." The idea of "justice" is therefore most strongly connected in Homer to the idea of vitality. "Anything that is beneficent for life cannot be injurious to God." For Homer, though, the arc of the universe does not bend toward justice. Life for humans is not a comedy, as it is for the immortal gods, but a tragedy. There is no redemption in the *Iliad*, only an inexorable fall, Bespaloff asserts, continuous "as the life-process itself which heads forever downward into death and the absurd." We can locate no innocence in *being*, as in Stoic moral reasoning, neither any innocence in *becoming*, as in Nietzsche's philosophy. There is only the All before which "Silence is the only answer, silence and that disabused, dispassionate look which the dying Hector casts on Achilles."

And herein lies the contradiction.

In contrast to Weil's subversive and antiheroic reading of the *Iliad*, Bespaloff identifies a clear hero in the epic: Hector, the archetypal "resistance hero," as over and against the "revenge hero" Achilles. It is not force but "the tragic confrontation of the revenge-hero and the resistance-hero [that] forms the *Iliad*'s true center." Bespaloff insists that it is hopeless to look in the *Iliad* for a condemnation of war, or for moral or political truths that can be expressed in terms other than the ineffable truth of the cosmos and of life itself. History, she writes, "is a show that neither knows divine justice nor asks for it." Yet Bespaloff proves incapable of practicing the moral detachment she commends in Homer. She admires

Hector, precisely as a man of virtue, more than any person or god in the poem. Hector is unique. Hector is not merely a cipher for raw force or inscrutable fate, but a free, courageous, and *gentle* man. Hector is the one who shows us how to be truly human in a universe of tragic absurdity.

Bespaloff's essay, Christopher Benfy points out, is hardly concerned with the actual scenes of battle that fill so much of the poem, and that Weil almost exclusively focuses on.[7] Instead, she presents a series of incisive and sympathetic character studies and philosophical musings, paying particular attention to women and to feminine perspectives on the war. It is Hector, though, who Bespaloff most often returns to as the archetypal Everyman who might teach us what to admire and how to live. Hector "is the guardian of the perishable joys" whose "zeal for glory exalts but does not blind him." He alone shows compassion to Helen without the taint of lust. His actions are marked by an existential "passion for defying destiny," even though he knows that fate in the end will have its way. "One omen is best, to fight for one's country," says Hector. Homer, according to Bespaloff, reveals a man's profoundest nature by showing us "his ways of loving and choosing his love." Hector's love is for his city and his family, and so is marked by a noble forgetfulness of self and the desire to preserve and protect. Achilles' love, by contrast, is an entirely narcissistic self-love; what he most adores in Patroclus is his own reflection. What he most relishes in life is the ecstasy of murder. Why should Hector's selfless love be preferred over Achilles' murderous egoism? Trapped within the cage of his own ego, Bespaloff suggests, Achilles may be an impressive force of nature. But he is also incapable of experiencing authentic joy in life, which requires the freedom of self-forgetfulness. It is in Hector alone that "the will to greatness never pits itself against the will to happiness."

Of course, Hector is not without his flaws. His prudence fails him on the eve of his confrontation with Achilles when he rejects Polydamas' counsel. He is not the strongest man in battle. He runs in terror from Achilles. But for Bespaloff, Hector's flaws are the necessary elements of his moral development and final heroism as Everyman. "Homer wanted him to be a whole man and spared him neither the quaking of terror nor the shame of cowardice." His flight from Achilles is in fact the flight of all humans from death, so that when at last Hector turns to face Achilles, he

---

7. Benfy, "Introduction," xxi.

teaches us how to face our own mortality: with self-mastery, with defiance, with resistance.

The Logic of Violence

"When Simone Weil called the *Iliad* 'The Poem of Force' and saw in it a commentary on the tragic futility of war, she was only partially right," George Steiner writes. "In the Homeric poem, war is valorous and ultimately ennobling. And even in the midst of carnage, life surges high."[8] Weil identifies moments of pity and compassion as the sole "luminous moments" or "moments of grace" in the poem. But this is too Christian a reading of Homer. "Homeric man's highest good is not the enjoyment of a quiet conscience, but the enjoyment of . . . public esteem," E. R. Dodds writes.[9] There are only two ways to achieve public esteem in the world of Hector, Ajax, and Achilles: in political counsel and in battle.

Weil, it seems to me, also overstates the "geometrical rigor" of Homer's universe. It is true that there is often a strict economy of fate at work in the poem, and the deaths of Patroclus, Hector, and Achilles are closely bound together in ways that suggest a common humanity and equality *among nobles*. Achilles unwittingly sends Patroclus to his death at Hector's hands wearing his armor, which Hector then strips from Patroclus' body and claims as his own. When Achilles slays Hector he therefore slays not only his enemy but also the image of his best friend and the image of himself. Past, present, and future, friend, enemy, and the self are all caught up as one. Yet the abuse heaped by Odysseus on the non-noble Thersites—who denounces the war in exactly the same terms as Achilles—never returns to Odysseus' head. In the world of the *Iliad*, there are few common standards by which to judge the actions of the strong and the weak. We thus often observe an asymmetry rather than a parallelism of force and suffering; fate never conspires to elevate commoners to the rank of kings. Bespaloff's non-pacific reading in this sense seems to me to be a more faithful exposition than Weil's of the actual text.

It would be a mistake, however, to judge either Weil's or Bespaloff's essays according to normal standards of literary interpretation. Their readings of Homer were not offered as detached and objective exercises

8. Steiner, *Tolstoy or Dostoevsky*, 77–78.
9. Dodds, *Greeks and the Irrational*, 17.

in literary criticism but as creative and even subversive re-readings of the *Iliad* under the weight of history. Weil's essay was "suffused with the sorrow she felt over the outbreak of World War II."[10] Bespaloff described her reflections on the poem as "my method of facing the war."[11] What the two writers were engaged in were imaginative revaluations of Homer in response to the unfolding crisis of totalitarianism. They sought to uncover new ways of thinking about violence and power in the present in the light of Homer's ancient and mythical past. If Bespaloff is more true to Homer's text in some ways than Weil, her praise of Hector is nevertheless equally conditioned by her fear of Nazism and her desire to encourage the forces of resistance. Both writers in this sense illustrate Steiner's statement that "Time . . . alters our view of a work or body of art."[12] Is it possible, after Auschwitz, to accept the destruction of a city and the genocide of its people as a mere stage for ennobling combat and glorious tales? For those who think not, Weil and Bespaloff's essays offer two possible ways of preserving and continuing to value the *Iliad* in a post-Holocaust world.

Allowing that Weil and Bespaloff are writing as much about history as about Homer, which of the two writers offers a more compelling reading of the *Iliad*? Although Weil pays little attention to Homer's political elitism or to the valorous aspects of combat in the *Iliad*, which are undeniably present (Weil may in fact have consciously suppressed key elements in the poem—such as Achilles' gentleness toward Priam—in order to intensify her theme of the dehumanizing effects of force[13]), her essay nevertheless remains to my mind the more trenchant and provocative essay on many levels. Early in the poem, the Greeks and Trojans agree that as a matter of piety and respect for ancient traditions they will each allow the other to collect and burn their dead without threat of attack. The pact seems aimed at placing certain moral boundaries or limits on the bloodshed. As the war intensifies, however, Homer depicts the combatants killing with increasing savagery until it is clear that no limits remain. By Book Fourteen of the poem, we find Greek and Trojan soldiers alike gleefully mutilating dead corpses as a way of humiliating their enemies. By the time Patroclus is killed by Hector at the end of Book Sixteen, the

---

10. Gray, *Simone Weil*, 156.
11. Bespaloff as cited in Benfy, "Introduction," xvii.
12. Steiner, *Language and Silence*, 8.
13. Benfy, "Introduction," xv.

Anarchy and Apocalypse

conflict has entered a phase of total war. Rules, conventions, earlier promises, venerable traditions—none can constrain the two sides, which now fight with unprecedented ferocity and savagery for the entirely irrational purpose of seizing Patroclus' dead body. The Trojans will fight to seize the dead body in order to further mutilate it and feed it to wild dogs. The Greeks will fight to prevent this humiliation at any cost. The idea that war might somehow be contained by heroic values of resistance, by prudential calculations, or by religious scruples such as those governing the burial of the dead, has been reduced to a shambles by the logic of violence and the internal dynamics of war by its very nature.

—2006

11 · *The Trial of God*

For Elie Wiesel

> Emblazoned over the gates of the world in which we live is the escutcheon of the demons. The mark of Cain in the face of man has come to overshadow the likeness of God. There have never been so much guilt and distress, agony and terror. At no time has the earth been so soaked with blood. Fellow men turned out to be evil ghosts, monstrous and weird. Ashamed and dismayed, we ask: Who is responsible?
>
> —Abraham Heschel[1]

In the summer of 1944 the gas chamber near the crematorium at Auschwitz went out of order. Because the other gas chambers were already filled with adults, the children were not gassed. Instead they were burned alive. There were several thousand of them. Occasionally one of the SS officers had pity on a child. He would beat its head against a stone until it was unconscious before placing the child on the wood. But this was not the regular way. Most of the children were simply thrown onto the pile. Then petrol, then wood, then more petrol. The pyre was finally set ablaze.[2] Who is responsible? In the face of unspeakable evil and unexplainable suffering, who, or what, is in control? For persons of belief the question leads to an insoluble dilemma: Why is God silent? The Creator watches children being burned but does not intervene. Why? How?

Let me tell you a story, says Elie Wiesel. The setting is Shamgorod, a Ukranian village in the year 1649. Three traveling minstrels, or *Purim*

---

1. Heschel, *Moral Grandeur and Spiritual Audacity*, 209.
2. Brown, *Elie Wiesel*, 27.

Anarchy and Apocalypse

spielers, arrive at the local inn on Purim eve. Purim is a festive holiday. It celebrates the escape of the Jews from genocide recorded in the book of Esther. The day is remembered with great storytelling, feasting, and merrymaking. Indeed, on Purim some Jews consider it a religious obligation to get drunk. Tradition also calls for the staging of a *Purimschpiel*, a humorous and satirical production retelling the tale of Jewish deliverance from the schemes of Haman. The three wandering minstrels hope to perform such a play for the Jews of the village in exchange for food and drink. When the innkeeper, Berish, learns of their plans, however, he laughs bitterly. Don't they know what town they are in? This is Shamgorod—*the* Shamgorod—site of a recent pogrom against the Jews. There is no audience for the players to perform before, for he and his daughter are the only Jews left alive. Nevertheless, the innkeeper declares, he will feed them if they agree to perform a play of his choosing. The play will be a *Din-Toïre*, a trial—the trial of God. Together they will indict the Creator for what He has done to the innkeeper's family, to the community of Shamgorod, to all Jews. The hungry actors agree. They will judge the case brought by the innkeeper against the Almighty. But first there is a problem that must be settled: who will defend God? None of the group is willing and it seems the trial will not occur after all. Suddenly a mysterious stranger appears who agrees to take the part, and so the trial begins.

Believers or Apostates: Who Lays the Charge?

The genesis of Wiesel's 1979 drama, *The Trial of God*, was an actual event he witnessed as a boy in Auschwitz. One night three masters of Jewish law and religion decided to convene a trial of the Lord of the Universe. In a barrack at the very heart of the liquidation the three rabbis called the Creator of Heaven and Earth to account for the massacre of His people. For several nights the case was heard. Witnesses were brought forward. Evidence was submitted. Finally a verdict was reached: the Lord God is guilty of crimes against His creation and against humanity. An immense silence followed the pronouncement until at last one of the scholars, looking at the sky, spoke. "It's time for evening prayers," he said. The members of the tribunal at once proceeded to recite *Maariv*, the evening service.[3] The event is both compelling and distressing. Hell has risen to the surface

---

3. Brown, "Introduction," in *Trial of God*, 6.

The Trial of God

of the earth and God offers no deliverance. Pharaoh has returned to his throne but Moses remains in heaven. Did the Almighty bring His children out of Egypt only to deliver them to Birkenau, Treblinka, Ravensbrück, Dachau? When God allows His chosen people to be turned to ash, how can humans not be anguished at the Divine Providence? How can we not protest against Him? But to place ourselves in *judgment* of God? To interrogate the Great I Am, whose ways are self-justified and beyond human understanding? Is this not the most perilous kind of presumption? Is this not blasphemy? Where were you, children of Auschwitz, when the foundations of earth were laid?

To understand the basis of the charge against God, it is important to try to grasp the enormity of the crime committed against His people in the *Shoah* to which Wiesel has given witness through his writing. The problems with any such attempt are clear. It is impossible for non-victims to comprehend save in all but the most limited of ways the experience of survivors. Yet the fates of all human beings are equally concerned with the question of God's presence, or absence, in human history. The attempt therefore must be made. We must try to understand and respond to what happened because our own destinies are inseparable from the destinies of the Jews of Auschwitz. Or the Jews of Shamgorod in Wiesel's allegory. "We will speak on behalf of the entire community," says Mendel, one of the three minstrels turned judge.[4] He is referring specifically to the Jewish community, but it is clear that all of humanity will share equally in the outcome of the case.

But then again, will they really? In Wiesel's play, Sam, the mysterious stranger who will defend God, raises his first objection. The accusers of God present their case as unique in history, as warranting our special concern, as having profound and universal implications, he argues. But is this a rational treatment of the facts of the human condition? What, after all, makes Shamgorod any more terrible or specious than every other holocaust or murder in earth's history? "What do you know of God that enables you to denounce Him?" Sam demands. "Think of our ancestors, who throughout centuries mourned over the massacre of their beloved ones and the ruin of their homes—and yet they repeated again and again that God's ways are just. Are we worthier than they were?"[5] There

---

4. Wiesel, *Trial of God*, 62.
5. Ibid., 133.

is clear logic to Sam's argument. <u>Suffering is suffering, regardless of the circumstances in which it occurs. Pain has a constant value—it does not undergo any qualitative alteration along with changes in time or setting.</u> How, then, can the innkeeper Berish condemn God when his brothers in other times—under equal, or even greater physical duress—did not? Surely, Sam suggests, this is evidence of a lack of constancy, a lack of faith; they did not question God and neither should we.

The matter of faith, and the loss of faith, is of critical importance. If God is dead, or if He never existed to begin with, there are no grounds for the trial to proceed; one cannot interview a corpse or prosecute a specter in a court of law. The significance and validity of the trial, as anything other than an intriguing but ultimately pointless exercise, therefore calls for an examination of the belief, or disbelief, of the prosecution. If Berish has broken faith with the Almighty, would this not be grounds for dismissing the charges altogether? The question requires that we leave Shamgorod temporarily and travel to a town called Sighet.

Sighet was a Jewish Shtetl in Carpathia where Wiesel lived as a child until March, 1944, when the terror began. The picture that emerges of this village in Wiesel's writing is one of a community rich in belief and fervent in devotion to the will of God. In his *Memoirs* and essays Wiesel introduces us to the Batizer Rebbe, a gentle old man with a snow-white beard who teaches the children of Sighet the Hebrew alphabet; Kalman, the Kabalist master who inducts Eliezer into the world of Jewish mysticism; Moshe the madman who weeps for God in exile and sings to welcome *Shabbat*; Eliezer's childhood friends, Moshe-Haim the cantor's son, Hershi whose sister drowned in the Iza River, and Itzu with whom he competes in everything including piety and devotion. There is also Maria, the Christian maid who celebrates Jewish holidays with the family; Grandma Nissel who questions Elie on his way home from *heder* about what he learned from the Bible each week; and Tsiporah, his golden-haired sister who studies at home because she is too young to go to school. And we witness Wiesel as a child, walking to synagogue with his father on Friday evening, their hands clasped, to welcome God's holy rest.

All at once the scene changes. There are dogs. There are men with clubs. Old people, women, children, beaten by gendarmes, German, Hungarian. Household items—furniture, books, clothing, pots, and pans—scattered in the street. The synagogue desecrated with vile placards. Blows followed by orders. A station. Waiting. Finally the trains. "Their shadow haunts my writing," Wiesel relates in his memoir *All Rivers Run to the Sea*. "They symbolize solitude, distress, and the relentless march of Jewish multitudes toward agony and death. I freeze every time I hear a train whistle."[6] It is not necessary to recount the events that followed, to travel with the trains and the Jews of Sighet to their final destination. Indeed, decency forbids it; for the goal of the trains was not a camp but a grave in the form of an oven, and Wiesel himself refuses to invade the privacy of the dead. "Let the gas chambers remain closed to prying eyes, and to the imagination," he writes. "Much has been said when silence ought to have prevailed. Let the dead speak for themselves, if they so choose. If not, may they be left in peace."[7]

Wiesel, however, was not killed. His family and his village perished, but somehow he survived the universe of the concentration camp. And while there are depths of depravation and inhumanity he refuses to ponder out of respect for the victims, his own experience he refuses to conceal or erase from memory. In *Night*, Wiesel's autobiography of Auschwitz, it is clear that at the heart of that experience was the shattering of his faith:

> Never shall I forget that night, the first night in camp, which has turned my life into one long night, seven times cursed and seven times sealed. Never shall I forget that smoke. Never shall I forget the little faces of the children, whose bodies I saw turned into wreaths of smoke beneath a silent blue sky.
>
> Never shall I forget those flames which consumed my faith forever.
>
> Never shall I forget that nocturnal silence which deprived me, for all eternity, of the desire to live. Never shall I forget those moments which murdered my God and my soul and turned my dreams to dust. Never shall I forget these things, even if I am condemned to live as long as God Himself. Never.[8]

How are we to respond to these often quoted but never less searing words? What do they mean for Wiesel and what must they mean to us? Did Auschwitz truly murder God? In that literal hell did the idea of transcendent goodness reveal itself to be nothing more than a hollow fiction? The idea of God's presence—His self-disclosure at Sinai—permeated the lives of the villagers of Sighet. Was Auschwitz the true revelation of histo-

6. Wiesel, *All Rivers Run to the Sea*, 74.
7. Ibid., 74.
8. Wiesel, *Night*, 44.

Anarchy and Apocalypse

ry—the revelation of His absence? Is this the drama behind the drama of Shamgorod? For many Jews the *Shoah* proved too terrible an event to allow for continued religious devotion. Wiesel's close friend Primo Levi delineated the crisis in terms of the nature of God's being: either God could not stop the killing and is therefore not God because not all-powerful, or He would not stop the killing and is therefore on the side of the killers. In either case, there is no longer any basis for belief in the God of scripture. "[T]he experience of the Lager with its frightful iniquity confirmed me in my non-belief," Levi writes. "It prevented, and still prevents me from conceiving of any form of providence or transcendent justice: Why were the moribund packed in cattle cars? Why were the children sent to the gas?"[9]

Wiesel, however, does not arrive at the same conclusion. He does not attempt to disprove the logic of Levi's argument. Rather, he simply states that while the Holocaust is not conceivable with God, neither is it conceivable without Him. "Theorists of the idea that 'God is dead' have used my words unfairly as justification of their rejection of faith," he writes. "[But] I have never renounced my faith in God. I have risen against His justice, protested His silence and sometimes His absence, but my anger rises up within faith and not outside it."[10] If the Holocaust consumed Wiesel's faith, then, it consumed his faith in the self-evident wisdom of God's ways—not in the fact of His existence. Wiesel does not ask *whether* God is; he asks *where* God is, *who* God is. Like Yossel Rakover in Zvi Kolitz's story of the Warsaw uprising, "Yossel Rakover's Appeal to God," Wiesel declares, "I believe in You, God of Israel, even though You have done everything to stop me from believing in You."[11] Indeed, this is why there must be a trial in Shamgorod—because God is *not* dead, because He is alive, and because, as Berish has charged, this is the most damning evidence against Him. "God is God, and I am only an innkeeper," he shouts. "But He will not prevent me from letting my anger explode! He will not succeed in stifling my truth."[12] Because of God's refusal to intervene, we must cry out. We must protest. We must scream our anguish. We must fill the universe

---

9. Levi, *Drowned and the Saved*, 145.
10. Wiesel, *All Rivers Run to the Sea*, 84.
11. Kolitz, "Yossel Rakover's Appeal to God," in *Out of the Whirlwind*, 396.
12. Wiesel, *Trial of God*, 42.

[handwritten note: can't this be done by an athiest?]

The Trial of God

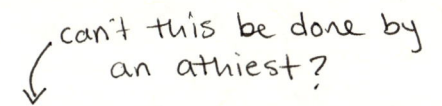

with our suffering until even the Creator cannot remain aloof. And if after this God is still silent? Surely then He is guilty as charged.

What Signifies the Silence of the Accused?

In the book of Job, the *Trial*'s most obvious literary precursor, Eliphaz, Bildad, Zophar, and Elihu counter Job's challenge to God by carefully restating the general principles of His providence and distributive justice. They represent themselves as voices of reason in distinction to Job's outrage. Sam's defense of God is in many ways a synthesis of their arguments. Similarly, in contrast to Berish's emotion filled accusations, Sam offers a dispassionate and reasoned defense of his Client. "I dislike emotions," he tells the court. "I prefer facts and cool logic."[13] The cool logic, he argues, is that the prosecution lacks the material proof necessary to back its charges. Human feeling, including suffering, is inconsequential for the purposes at hand, for pain "does not constitute judicial evidence." Berish, Sam declares, must offer more to the court than his own anger. He must offer some physical finding that irrefutably implicates the Almighty in the tragedy of Shamgorod. Berish is infuriated at Sam's prevarication. There are no more Jews in Shamgorod, he points out. What greater proof is needed? Where once there was a community, families, songs, synagogues, there is nothing. Is this not evidence enough of God's hostility or indifference to the fate of man? "Shamgorod is mute. Its silence—what is it if not a fact?" he says. "Over a hundred Jewish families lived here; now there is one—and this one is mutilated, maimed, deprived of joy and hope. What is all this to you—and Him? What is this, I'm asking you?"[14] Sam nevertheless insists that the prosecution call forth witnesses to testify. Berish cannot comply for obvious reasons: the witnesses are all dead. Yet this, he declares, is itself the most powerful testimony possible:

> I implore the court to consider their absence as the weightiest of proofs, as the heaviest of accusations. They are witnesses, Your Honor, invisible and silent witnesses, but still witnesses! Let their testimony enter your conscience and your memory! Let their premature, unjust deaths turn into an outcry so forceful that it will make the universe tremble with fear and remorse![15]

13. Ibid., 122.
14. Ibid., 127–28.
15. Ibid., 129–30.

Anarchy and Apocalypse

In *The Drowned and the Saved* Primo Levi likewise draws attention to the testimony of the dead. Survivors, he maintains, are not the true witnesses of the *Shoah*; for no matter the suffering they endured, they did not reach the bottom of the horror contained in the camps. "Those who did so, those who saw the Gorgon, have not returned to tell about it," he writes. Yet these, the submerged, are "the complete witnesses, the ones whose deposition would have a general significance."[16] Survivors are the exception; the dead are the rule. Their silence, then, is the most complete description of what happened. In the shadow of Auschwitz speech betrays truth. Words fail to bear adequate testimony.

This fact necessitates a reconsideration of the conceptual framework of Western thought. To the Western mind silence is devoid of meaning. It suggests chaos, the formlessness described in the second verse of Genesis which preceded the Creation. Our Greek-Judaic heritage is based upon conceptions of *Logos*—Reason or the Divine Word—by which all reality is ordered. As a result, our experience with truth is almost exclusively verbal in character. Western literature, philosophy, theology, art and history all seek to enclose truth within the categories of rational discourse.[17] Berish's insistence that *absence* and *silence* are in fact a presence and a witness in the trial thus marks a step outside the bounds of both Jewish (excluding certain of its mystical expressions) and classical Western thought. It implies a powerful negation of any normal mode of communication to confront the reality of the inhuman, whether in Shamgorod or in the concentration camps of the twentieth century. Because only the dead have the right to speak, we must learn to listen to their silence, to hear their absent voices.

There are ways of thinking which recognize meaning in silence. In Buddhist and Taoist metaphysics the loftiest contemplative act is that which leaves language behind. The ineffable lies beyond the strictures of time and therefore beyond the realm of spoken words. Silence, in the Eastern view, conveys the intimation of God.[18] Another example of the dynamic power of silence may be found in the sphere of music. The elements of a musical composition include not only sounds but also "rests." Without the order brought to a piece of music by these silences, the work

---

16. Levi, *Drowned and the Saved*, 83–84.
17. Steiner, *Language and Silence*, 11–12.
18. Ibid., 13.

The Trial of God

cannot sound as its author intended. The silence between the notes communicates to us just as surely as the notes between the silences.[19] But is the silence of the dead loud enough to convey the enormity of the crime? Is the outrage of their absence sufficient witness to the shame of modern history? The question becomes more pressing as the *Shoah* recedes from us in time; for where the absence of Jewish communities in Eastern Europe may have initially served as a powerful testimony to the event, this same absence now makes possible collective amnesia and even bold-faced denial. When Cain murdered Abel, the Genesis writer tells us, his blood—his silence—screamed out to God from the ground. Yet when the act is repeated six million times, God hears nothing; His own silence, in collusion with the silence of the world, drowns out the silence of the dead.

This universal silence, André Neher suggests, makes the *Shoah* unlike any other event in history. At Hiroshima, Dresden and Coventry events were clamorous. There were free witnesses present to observe and report what happened. There were almost immediate attempts at assistance. The cry of suffering gripped the world. More recently, in Bosnia and Rwanda, we have watched atrocities unfold in real time through the omnipresent eye of the modern media. "But at Auschwitz," writes Neher, "everything unfolded, was fulfilled and accomplished for weeks, months, and years on end in absolute silence, away from and out of the mainstream of history."[20] It is true that there are other examples of mass liquidation, such as that in Stalinist Russia—though never on equal scale motivated purely by racial and religious hatred. It is true that there have been other cases of genocide—though even in Cambodia and Rwanda not systematized and methodically planned murder employing the vast material resources, technology, energy and ingenuity of a modern industrialized superpower. And it is true that there are other cases of slavery—though even in its most cruel manifestations not slavery which viewed the slave as a consumable raw material to be expended in the process of manufacture: gold teeth for the treasury, hair for mattresses, ashes for road fill and fertilizer. But never, given the scale and intent of the crime, has the silence of the universe been more complete or disturbing as during the *Shoah*.

---

19. Brown, *Elie Wiesel*, 31.
20. Neher, "Silence of Auschwitz," in *Holocaust*, 10.

Anarchy and Apocalypse

Wiesel's novel, *The Town Beyond the Wall*, addresses the issue of the silence of the world throughout the Holocaust. The story tells of Michael, a survivor of the concentration camps, who travels to his home village in Hungary to confront "the face in the window"—the face of an anonymous stranger who watched placidly as the Jews were deported. This silent bystander, Wiesel suggests, embodies evil even more than the killers. For indifference is even less human than hatred. "Your duty was clear," Michael says to the silent stranger, "you had to choose. To fight us or to help. In the first case I would have hated you; in the second, loved. You never left your window: I have only contempt for you."[21] The face in the window symbolizes all those who stood by and watched the *Shoah* without resisting or bearing witness.

There are, then, different kinds of silence. There is a silence that testifies and sanctifies and a silence which desecrates and denies. This leads to a wrenching paradox for survivors, and indeed, for all concerned human beings: the event is too terrible to speak, and the event is too terrible not to speak. Job says "Though I speak, my grief is not relieved; And if I remain silent, how am I eased?" (Job 16.6) Who is Job if not a survivor? Who if not, as Wiesel writes in *Messengers of God*, our contemporary?[22] The great novelists who lived through the Holocaust—Camus, Silone, Mauriac, Faulkner—did not write about it; they avoided it out of respect for the dead and concern for the truth. For the first ten years after the end of the war Wiesel imposed upon himself a vow of silence for similar reasons, so terrible was the event. At last he wrote *Night*, originally titled *And the World Was Silent*, which remains his only book to speak directly of his experience of the *Shoah*, though all of his works in some way deal with its implications. Why did he finally do so? In *A Jew Today* Wiesel declares that the mere fact of survival imposed a sacred duty to testify. "[N]ot to remember was equivalent to becoming the enemy's accomplice: whosoever contributes to oblivion finishes the Killer's work. Hence the vital necessity to bear witness lest one find oneself in the enemy's camp."[23] This role of witness and messenger, Primo Levi writes, compels survivors to speak. It marks the center of their entire existence. "They speak

---

21. Wiesel, *Town Beyond the Wall*, 160.
22. Wiesel, *Messengers of God*, 211–35.
23. Wiesel, *A Jew Today*, 199.

The Trial of God

because they know they are witnesses in a trial of planetary and epochal dimensions."[24]

And yet, Wiesel insists, whatever is written about the Holocaust remains provisional and incomplete. Between words and truth there is an unbridgeable gulf. Consequently, there can be no such thing as a Holocaust literature. "Auschwitz," he writes, "negates all literature as it negates all theories and doctrines; to lock it into a philosophy means to restrict it. To substitute words, any words, for it is to distort it. A Holocaust literature? The very term is a contradiction."[25] Wiesel's art is a reflection of this conviction. He writes in a sparse, lean prose in which what is not said is as important as what is. "It is the style of the chroniclers of the ghettos," he says, "where everything had to be said swiftly, in one breath. You never knew when the enemy might kick in the door, sweeping us away into nothingness. Every phrase was a testament. There was no time or reason for anything superfluous."[26] According to Hasidic tradition, the white spaces in the Torah are God-given as well as the words. We must read Wiesel with this view in mind. We must also understand Berish's charge against God in these terms. The testimony of the dead, like the white spaces in the Bible, impose an order and a weight to history. The absence of Jews in Shamgorod is a real and vital presence in the trial as Berish asserts. Their silence is a silence that bears witness. But what about the silence of the Almighty? If there are two kinds of silence—one that testifies and one that denies—the question that must be decided by the court is, Which kind of silence is the silence of God? That of a Victim? Or that of an Executioner?

Is the Creator Mad, Blessed Be His Name?

According to the Christian priest of Shamgorod, the reason the Jews suffer is because they are under God's judgment and curse. "God doesn't love you anymore," he tells the minstrels and innkeeper. "He has turned His face away from you. Why don't you see the truth as it is? He is fed up with you. He is disgusted with you." This rejection, he claims, is the penalty of God upon the Jewish race for having rejected Christ:

24. Levi, *Drowned and the Saved*, 149.
25. Wiesel, *A Jew Today*, 197.
26. Wiesel, *All Rivers Flow to the Sea*, 321.

From now on, we shall be your masters, your rulers; we shall be your God. Why should we be invested with such powers if it were not for God, who entrusted us with a mission to you, His rebellious children? It is the will of God that we, Christians, shall be your God.[27]

The priest's view of the Jewish people is more or less an exact expression of the attitudes of the Christian church, both Catholic and Protestant, toward Jews through hundreds of years. Indeed, from the consolidation of Christianity and the Roman Empire under Constantine until the modern period, anti-Semitism was an integral feature of Christian doctrine. The reasons for the development of this anti-Jewish theology are not difficult to discern.[28] First, the fact that Jews interpreted the Hebrew Bible—which Christianity also embraced—differently from Christians was a threat to the exclusive scriptural authority claimed by church leaders. If the Jews understood Scripture correctly, Christian explanations might be wrong. Hence, to ensure that the laity responded to the rites and symbols of religion only as prescribed by ecclesiastical authorities, it was necessary for clerics to convince all Christians that all Jews were in error. Second, the fact that Jews rejected the deity of Christ suggested that either He was not the Messiah or that the people of God were no longer His people. Because the former possibility could not be countenanced, Christians wholeheartedly embraced the latter view. The persistence of the Jewish faith, they concluded, was merely evidence of the magnitude of their rebellion against the will of God. Finally, Christians held all Jews for all time accountable for Christ's death. It was the corporate Jewish nation, they maintained, which rejected and killed Jesus. Their continued rejection of the Lordship of Christ through history therefore implicated them in the crime of their forebears. Hebrews were not merely rebels to God's will; they were in a very real sense "Christ-killers." Had not the mobs that crucified Jesus declared "His blood shall be on us *and on our children*"? (Matt 27:25).

In his novel, *The Gates of the Forest*, Wiesel exposes the seeds of hatred contained in these beliefs. Gregor is a young boy hiding from the Germans. To avoid capture he travels to a village where the old family servant, Maria, takes him into hiding. Assuming the role of her deaf mute

---

27. Wiesel, *Trial of God*, 98.
28. See Goldhagen, *Hitler's Willing Executioners*, 50.

nephew, Gregor manages to avoid rousing the suspicions of the other villagers. However, when the local school puts on a passion play of Christ's death, their loathing for Jews is manifested with devastating consequences. Gregor is inadvertently cast in the role of Judas, the paradigmatic Jew who betrayed Christ. As the drama unfolds, the actors portraying the other disciples, as well as the audience, decide to punish Judas for his crime against the Savior. "'Judas! Traitor!'" they scream. "'Judas! You did it for money!' 'You betrayed the Son of God!' 'You killed the Savior!' 'You thought you could get away? There's no escape from the wrath of God!'"[29] The villagers crowd about Gregor and, as their frenzy increases, begin to beat him savagely. "'He's got to confess!' 'He's got to repent!'" they howl. "'Let justice be done! Vengeance! He who sent Christ to death deserves to die.'"[30] The attack is ritualistic in nature. In it we see the translation of poisonous ideas into a murderous and bloody rite of expiation. The theater of condemnation thus serves as prelude to the pogrom of elimination. So it was in Sighet, Wiesel recalls in his memoirs, where on Christmas Eve the Christian children of the village put on masks and took up whips to stage "the hunt for the Jews"—a hunt which soon turned deadly earnest.

There were, it should be noted, exceptions to the rule of Christian complicity in murder. Wiesel's family housekeeper, a Christian named Maria, begged his parents to hide their family in a remote cabin she owned. They declined the offer because they did not think the rumors of the coming terror could be true. Wiesel pays tribute to this woman, and gentiles like her, in Maria, the maid in *The Gates of the Forest*, and in the maid in *The Trial of God*, also named Maria. Besides the courage of individual Christians during the Holocaust there were also some cases of Christian communities acting in solidarity with Jews. Philip Hallie tells of the Huguenot village of Le Chambon-sur-Lignon in the Cévennes Mountains of southeastern France, that sheltered and saved about 6,000 Jews. An incident which occurred there early in 1941 illustrates the corporate attitude of the Chambonnais peasants toward the Jewish people—an attitude grounded in the Anabaptist tradition of religious dissent and the radical ethics of nonviolence. One afternoon a shawled refugee woman appeared at the door of a farmhouse in the town. The farm-woman who answered the door invited her inside where it was warm. The refugee entered and,

---

29. Wiesel, *Gates of the Forest*, 101.
30. Ibid., 104–5.

in heavily accented French, asked the villager for eggs for her children. "Are you Jewish?" the woman asked the refugee. For most Jews the question led to certain deportation and death. The woman began to tremble. Nevertheless, she answered truthfully: "Yes." The Chambonnais woman left the terrified refugee in the kitchen and ran to the stairs. "Husband, children, come down, come down!" she cried. "We have in our house at this very moment a representative of the Chosen People!"[31]

The story attests to the fact that there were some Christians who did not accept the theology of God's rejection of the Jews. These individuals saw the covenant relationship between God and Israel as eternal and unique, and therefore in some sense still operative; or they saw the Jewishness of the persecuted as irrelevant and responded with compassion toward them as fellow human beings. But can such examples outweigh the burden of evil directly linked to the masses of professing Christians? Given the millions of Christians who either condoned or actively participated in the liquidation, can such cases be seen as anything other than anomalies of belief, than as aberrations in the faith? In general, there was an inverse ratio in Europe between the presence of fundamentalist Christianity and the survival of Jews during the Holocaust period.[32] Not all victims were Jews and not all Christians were killers. But, Wiesel writes in *A Jew Today*, the opposite remains a harsh fact: "in Auschwitz all the Jews were victims, all the killers were Christian."[33] They came from Christian homes. They had received Christian education. They attended confession between the massacres. As a *people* those claiming to be followers of Jesus explained and justified the destruction of the Jews as a matter of belief.

Hundreds of statements made by Christian leaders of nearly every denomination, from Catholics to Seventh-day Adventists, testify to this fact. Two examples will suffice to illustrate. First, in 1942 the Nietra Rebbe visited the Archbishop Kametko to beg for Catholic intervention in the deportation of Slovakian Jews. The Rebbe did not know of the gas chambers and so in his plea stressed the dangers of hunger and disease for children and the elderly. The Archbishop replied:

> It is not just a matter of deportation. You will not die there of hunger and disease. They will slaughter all of you there, old and

31. Hallie, "From Cruelty to Goodness," in *Vice and Virtue in Everyday Life*, 18.
32. Greenberg, "Cloud of Smoke, Pillar of Fire," in *Holocaust*, 308.
33. Wiesel, *A Jew Today*, 11.

The Trial of God

young alike, women and children, at once—it is the punishment that you deserve for the death of our Lord and Redeemer, Jesus Christ—you have only one solution. Come over to our religion and I will work to annul this decree.[34]

Again, in 1948, when it was universally known what had taken place during the *Shoah*, the German Evangelical Conference at Darmstadt proclaimed that the suffering of the Jews was a divine visitation and called upon the Jewish people to cease their ongoing crucifixion of Christ and convert to Christianity.[35]

How, Irving Greenberg asks, can one morally be a Christian after this? "Is not the faith of a gospel of love ... fatally tainted with collaboration with genocide—conscious or unconscious?"[36] Wiesel likewise asks whether the wager of faith in Jesus was lost during the *Shoah*. "How are we to explain the passivity of the population as it watched the persecution of its Jews," he writes. "How explain that the Christian in them did not make their arms tremble as they shot at children or their conscience bridle as they shoved their naked, beaten victims into the factories of death?"[37] The problem for both writers is not the person Jesus Christ—it is what His followers have done with Him. In the trial in Shamgorod the minstrel Mendel says, "I speak not of Christ but of those who betray Him. They invoke His teaching to justify their murderous deeds. His true disciples would behave differently; there are no more around. There are no more Christians in this Christian land."[38] In *Conversations* with Harry James Cargas, Wiesel says, "I believe that the Christians betrayed Christ more than the Jews did."[39] Even so, can the destiny of Jesus be separated from the deeds of His followers? "As far as Jews are concerned," states Wiesel, "he may be retroactively guilty for all the murders and massacres that were done in his name."[40] "Golgotha," he writes in *Messengers of God*, "has served as pretext for countless massacres of sons and fathers cut down together by sword and fire in the name of a word that considered itself

---

34. Ibid., 308.
35. Ibid., 309.
36. Ibid., 310.
37. Wiesel, *A Jew Today*, 12.
38. Wiesel, *Trial of God*, 99.
39. *Harry James Cargas in Conversation with Elie Wiesel*, 48.
40. Ibid., 48.

141

Anarchy and Apocalypse

synonymous with love."[41] The question, then, which confronts us is, Does the balance of justice still tip in favor of the good done for Jesus' sake? Or have the actions of Christ's self-proclaimed followers ultimately invalidated the witness of His life? This is the crisis of modern Christianity—the crisis of association with the crucifiers rather than the Crucified.

As important as these issues are, in Wiesel's drama they are not Berish's concern. Jesus is not the One who stands accused in Shamgorod. Nor do the priest's claims—that the suffering of the Jews is God's curse on them for having rejected Christ—hold much authority in this Jewish court of law. He exits the inn having failed to win any converts. Still, the central theme of the priest's argument remains; namely, that God either allows or sends suffering as a penalty for sin. Sam seems to agree. "Jews are being judged," he offers in defense of the Accused. It is not a new suggestion. The prophets of the Hebrew Bible often declared that the sufferings of Israel were the result of transgressions against the Almighty. The author of the book of Lamentations, for example, attributes the devastation of Israel—including the rape of women and the slaughter and starvation of children—to the wrath of God. During the Roman era Jewish rabbis agreed that the Fall of Jerusalem was a divine punishment. If we do not deny the biblical testimony and heritage of the Jewish faith, then, we must consider the possibility that the *Shoah* was a manifestation of God's judgment on His people.

The problem with such a schema of divine justice is that, instead of defending or explaining God's ways, it only makes them appear more capricious and unjust. For if suffering is God's punishment for sin, the converse should also be true; devotion to God ought to in some way shield the faithful from the penalties inflicted on the wayward. Yet the history of the Lagers reveals the opposite tendency. "The 'saved' of the Lager," Primo Levi writes, "were not the best, those predestined to do good, the bearers of a message: what I had seen and lived through proved the exact contrary. Preferably the worst survived, the selfish, the violent, the insensitive, the collaborators . . . the spies."[42] Ruthlessness—among the victims as well as the executioners—was rewarded, while devotion to God and concern for one's neighbor generally increased the likelihood that one

---

41. Wiesel, *Messengers of God*, 76.
42. Levi, *Drowned and the Saved*, 82.

The Trial of God

would meet destruction. God's defenders?, asks Berish—"He killed them! He massacred His friends and allies!"[43]

In his collection of essays, *Legends of Our Time,* Wiesel tells of his first Yom Kippur, the Day of Atonement, in camp. For several weeks before the occasion, learned rabbis gathered every night to transcribe by memory the appropriate prayers to be recited. These were then distributed to cantors so that each barracks might function as its own synagogue. The Holy Day arrived and services proceeded as planned. However, Wiesel recalls, as the prayers were offered the words all rang false. They did not seem to concern the Jews anymore. "*Ashannu*, we have sinned. *Begadnu*, we have betrayed. *Gazalnu*, we have stolen. What? Us? *We* have sinned? Against whom? By doing what? *We* have betrayed? Whom?"[44]

Why, Wiesel asks, did Jews—including himself—ask for forgiveness for the guilt of their executioners? Why did they take responsibility for sins and crimes they had neither the desire nor the power of committing? "Perhaps we felt guilty despite everything," he writes. "Things were simpler that way. It was better to believe our punishments had meaning, that we had deserved them; to believe in a cruel but just God was better than not to believe at all." The condemned thus praised the Almighty for chastising their sins. "You are our God, blessed be your name," they cried. "You smite us without pity, you shed our blood, we give thanks to you for it, O Eternal One, for you are determined to show us that you are just and that your name is justice!"[45] Can we say Amen to these prayers of contrition from the lips of the forsaken? Or do they cause our consciences, like Wiesel's, to revolt? In order for a punishment to be just it must be proportional to the error committed. Can we discern any such proportion between the suffering inflicted during the *Shoah* and any conceivable transgression, even against the Almighty?

I cannot. In Auschwitz newborn babies were tattooed. What failing, what sin possibly legitimizes this kind of sadism? The sins of the child? The idea is absurd. The sins of the parents? Reason tells us that this would not be just at all. We sense that extolling God's justice in the shadow of the Holocaust only heaps shame, not honor, on His name. If the crematorium is the Creator's judgment on humankind, He is mad, blessed be His name.

---

43. Wiesel, *Trial of God*, 103.
44. Wiesel, *Legends of Our Time*, 59–60.
45. Ibid., 60.

Anarchy and Apocalypse

We might circumvent these questions altogether by declaring that God is not subject to the same principles of justice as humans, that because He is God His ways are by definition just and good and unquestionable. This is precisely what Sam argues in the trial. Above and beyond human justice, he declares, is the justice of God. But Berish rejects this defense. "I want no part of a justice that escapes me, diminishes me and makes a mockery out of mine! Justice is here for men and women—I therefore want it to be human, or let Him keep it!"[46]

Behind Berish's outburst is a stubborn logic. If Divine and human justice are in different categories, as Sam claims, to speak of the injustice of God may be impossible. But, by the same token, to speak of the justice of God would be meaningless. Either God's justice and human justice are ultimately of the same order, or neither truly exists as far as the other is concerned. God's defenders must therefore explain Shamgorod and Auschwitz in terms other than judgment. If He is a just God He is *not* the Divine Executor, the one issuing rewards for faithfulness and tribulations as a punishment for sin—at least not in the present. Where, then, is He to be found in the drama of human suffering? Surely He is not a neutral bystander. "Would a father stand by quietly, silently, and watch his children being slaughtered?" asks Berish.[47]

Or Is the Lord of the Universe Also a Survivor of Our Ways?

At last Sam offers his most compelling defense of God. "When human beings kill one another, where is God to be found? You see Him among the killers. I find Him among the victims," he says. If this is true, how can Berish accuse Him? Shall a victim denounce one who shares in his suffering? It is hard to conceive of guilt where there is solidarity. The suffering of God is an integral theme in Jewish belief. In his *Memoirs* Wiesel recounts a Midrashic tale to illustrate this understanding. When the Almighty comes to restore the children of Israel from their exile, he writes, they will say to Him: "Master of the Universe, it is You who dispersed us among the nations, driving us from Your abode, and now it is You who bring us back. Why is that?" God will reply with a parable:

---

46. Wiesel, *Trial of God*, 123.
47. Ibid., 128.

> One day a king drove his wife from his palace, and the next day he had her brought back. The queen, astonished, asked him: "Why did you send me away yesterday only to bring me back today?" "Know this," replied the king, "that I followed you out of the palace, for I could not live in it alone[48]

So, God tells the children of Israel, "Having seen you leave my abode, I left it too, that I might return with you." The Lord of the Universe accompanies His children into exile, into suffering. We are partners in banishment. The Almighty, the *Shekinah,* is an outcast, writes Abraham Joshua Heschel. "God is in captivity in this world, in the oblivion of our lives."[49] What touches us therefore also moves Him; what happens to God reaches us. He is never absent from His creation, even in the kingdom of night. "We suffer for the same reasons and ascribe the same coefficient to our common hope," writes Wiesel. What is this hope? That because God and humanity participate in the same drama we will ultimately share the same destiny; that God and Israel will together find deliverance.

In *The Gates of the Forest,* Gregor, who manages to escape death when the rest of his village is destroyed, struggles with a sense of guilt common among survivors: that to live is to betray the dead. "The injustice perpetrated in an unknown land concerns me; I am responsible," he concludes. "He who is not among the victims is with the executioners."[50] But Yehuda, a resistance fighter who senses his own imminent death, chides Gregor for turning his suffering inward into despair. "This is the time to love," he says. "An act of love may tip the balance."[51] Gregor is angered by the suggestion of love in the midst of suffering, in the mouth of the void, but Yehuda does not relent:

> It's inhuman to wall yourself up in pain and memories as if in a prison. Suffering must open us to others. It must not cause us to reject them. The Talmud tells us that God suffers with man. Why? In order to strengthen the bonds between creation and the creator; God chooses to suffer in order to better understand man and be better understood by him.[52]

---

48. Wiesel, *All Rivers Run to the Sea,* 103.
49. Heschel, *Moral Grandeur and Spiritual Audacity,* 260.
50. Wiesel, *Gates of the Forest,* 166.
51. Ibid., 176.
52. Ibid., 178–79.

Anarchy and Apocalypse

At the heart of the Divine-human encounter is solidarity in sorrow. Our anguish is not like a stone cast into a canyon, but a bridge across an abyss; at one end stands humanity, at the other waits God.

How does the Jewish understanding of the suffering of God differ from the Christian view of the suffering of Christ? In both Catholicism and Protestantism, sharing in the suffering of Jesus has often been seen as the prerequisite of Christian living. In *The Cost of Discipleship,* Dietrich Bonhoeffer writes that "Just as Christ is Christ only in virtue of his suffering and rejection, so the disciple is a disciple only in so far as he shares his Lord's suffering and rejection and crucifixion . . . When Christ calls a man He bids him come and die."[53] Kierkegaard maintained that in order to be a Christian one was required to hate life in this world and to accept suffering as an act of submission to the will of God. As Sonya tells Raskolnikov in Dostoevsky's *Crime and Punishment,* "You must accept suffering and redeem yourself by it."[54] Judaism, by contrast, has not generally taught that suffering is desirable or necessary for belief. In the Jewish tradition, life in this world is precious and must be cherished and defended since only here can we carry out a *mitzvah,* a divine commandment, in service to the Lord.[55] Humanity is redeemed in spite of, not because of, suffering. The response of the Hebrew prophets to tribulation therefore includes submission, but also protest. "Why do You forget us forever? Why do You forsake us so long?" (Lam 5:20).

We can distinguish, then, between the suffering of God in the Jewish faith and the Christian view of the passion of Christ. For where the significance of the passion story—at least according to some Christian thinkers—is seen in the concept of *imitatio,* a model or pattern for practical living, the suffering of God in Judaism is based upon what Abraham Heschel refers to as divine *pathos,* the fact that God is emotionally affected by human conduct.[56] We are not called to imitate or share in the suffering of God. Rather, we are conscious that God feels the suffering of people. He is bound to us by chords of sympathy.

It may be that passion and pathos are not mutually exclusive traits of God's character. Christians might embrace Christ's witness of self-sacrific-

---

53. Bonhoeffer, *Cost of Discipleship,* 96, 99.
54. Dostoevsky, *Crime and Punishment,* 489.
55. Ibid., 251.
56. Heschel, *Prophets, Volume II,* 99–103.

The Trial of God

ing love while at the same time affirming the goodness and sanctity of life on earth, the revelation of the Hebrew Bible, the holiness of the Sabbath, the greatness of the Mosaic law and faith in the God of Abraham. This, I believe, would be an authentic Christianity, true to its Hebraic roots, to the deepest meaning of the Gospels, and to the Jewishness of Christ. Still, those who hold to the doctrine of *imitatio Christi* must weigh the question: has Christian theology run aground of human history? For if persecution and suffering is the mark of the "true" church, as the apostles and Protestant reformers believed, in this century the true church is surely a synagogue. The suffering of Jesus finds parallel not in the collective suffering of Christians, but in the experience of Eastern European Jews.

A Commentary in Documents

Now the chief priests and all the council sought testimony against Jesus to put Him to death, but found none. For many bore false witness against Him, but their testimonies did not agree:

> The hunger for long knives becomes a yell.
>
> The street is a volcano of hate.
>
> The mob whinnies around the longed-for gallows.
>
> The Jew is the world's plague.
>
> A dog's fury is too mild for them.
>
> Jewish justices betray with dark relationships.
>
> In their cures, Jewish pharmacists pour poison and infection.
>
> They are usurers, bloodsuckers, every one.
>
> Drive their children from the schools,
>
> Their orphans from their orphan homes,
>
> And their sick out of the hospitals—Abraham Heschel, 1933[57]

Some began to spit on Him, and to blindfold Him, and to beat Him, and to say to Him, "Prophesy!" And the officers struck Him with the palms of their hands . . . Then the soldiers led Him away into the hall called Praetorium and they called together the whole garrison:

---

57. Heschel, *Moral Grandeur and Spiritual Audacity*, 71.

Anarchy and Apocalypse

> Every day large coaches come to the ghetto; they take soldiers through as if it was a zoo. It is the thing to do to provoke the wild animals. Often soldiers strike out at passers-by with long whips as they drive through. They go to the cemetery where they take pictures. They compel the families of the dead and the rabbis to interrupt the funeral and to pose in front of their lenses. They set up genre pictures (old Jew above the corpse of a girl)—Report by the Polish government in exile, 1942[58]

And when they had mocked Him, they . . . led Him out to crucify Him:

> The convoys that transported Polish Jews from ghettos to Lagers, or from Lager to Lager, contained up to a hundred and twenty persons per car: their journey was brief . . . Now, fifty persons in a freight car is most uncomfortable; they can all lie down simultaneously to rest, but body against body. If they are one hundred or more, even a trip of a few hours is an inferno: one must take turns standing or squatting, and often, among the travelers, there are old people, sick people, children, nursing women, lunatics, or individuals who go mad during or because of the journey—Primo Levi, *The Drowned and the Saved*[59]

He was led as a lamb to the slaughter, and as a sheep before its shearers is silent, So He opened not His mouth:

> On the corner stands a tough SS man who tells the poor people in a pastoral voice: "Nothing is going to happen to you" . . . And so they climb the little staircase and then they see it all: mothers with children at the breasts, little naked children, adults, men, women, all naked. They hesitate but they enter the death chambers, driven on by the others behind them or by the leather whips of the SS, the majority without saying a word—Kurt Gerstein, SS officer at Belzec, 1942[60]

And when they crucified Him, they divided His garments, casting lots for them to determine what every man should take:

> The first consignment of 1,500 suits . . . delivered by you are so poor in quality that the majority cannot be used for our welfare purposes. Moreover, your consignment does not contain complete suits but only unmatched jackets and pairs of trousers. A large

---

58. Noakes and Pridham, *Nazism, 1919–1945*, Vol. 3, 1069.
59. Levi, *Drowned and the Saved*, 108.
60. Noakes and Pridham, *Nazism, 1919–1945*, 1151.

The Trial of God

> number of the pieces of clothing are covered in spots and some are stained with dirt and blood ... in the case of 51 jackets out of 200 the Jewish star has not been removed! ... I hope that you understand my complaints and appreciate that we cannot donate such poor pieces of clothing to our returnees but only good ones—Letter from the Winter Aid Programme in the Wartheland to the ghetto administration in Lódz, 1943[61]

And the inscription of His accusation was written above: THE KING OF THE JEWS:

> Just next to the small station with two platforms there was a large barrack, the so-called "Cloak Room", with a large counter for valuables ... Then a small path in the open air under birch trees, enclosed by a double fence of barbed wire to right and left with signs up: "To the inhalation and bath rooms" ... On the far wall, not clearly visible in the darkness, large wooden stage-type doors. On the roof, as a little practical joke the Star of David!—Kurt Gerstein, SS officer at Belzec, 1942[62]

Two robbers were crucified with Him, one on the right and another on the left ... And at the ninth hour Jesus cried out with a loud voice, saying "Eloi, Eloi, lama sabachthani?" which is translated, "My God, My God, why have you forsaken me?":

> The three necks were placed at the same moment within the nooses.
> "Long live liberty!" cried the two adults
> But the child was silent.
> "Where is God? Where is He?" someone behind me asked.
> At a sign from the head of the camp, the three chairs tipped over.
> Total silence throughout the camp. On the horizon, the sun was setting.
> "Bare your heads!" yelled the head of the camp. His voice was raucous. We were weeping.
> "Cover your heads!"
> Then the march past began. The two adults were no longer alive. Their tongues hung swollen, blue-tinged. But the third rope was still moving; being so light, the child was still alive ...

---

61. Ibid., 1171–72.
62. Ibid., 1151.

Anarchy and Apocalypse

> For more than half an hour he stayed there, struggling between life and death, dying in slow agony under our eyes. And we had to look him full in the face. He was still alive when I passed in front of him. His tongue was still red, his eyes not yet glazed.
>
> Behind me, I heard the same man asking: "Where is God now?"
>
> And I heard a voice within me answer him: "Where is He? Here He is—He is hanging here on this gallows."—Elie Wiesel, *Night*

The Argument from Freedom

Having said that God suffers, and that His suffering parallels human suffering, what have we proved as far as the trial in Shamgorod is concerned? According to Berish, nothing. As true as these statements may be, he insists, there is an essential difference between the suffering of God and that of humanity: His suffering is voluntary, humanity's is not. "He—a victim?" Berish asks. "A victim is powerless; is He powerless? He is almighty, isn't He? He could use His might to save the victims, but he doesn't!"[63] God cannot be a victim in the same sense that humans are; for while He may elect to suffer, when humans suffer they may only elect to endure. What, then, is the point of God's suffering? Why does He make Himself vulnerable? To understand us better? To allow us to understand Him? How does understanding pain make it any easier to bear? Reason tells us that the suffering of one does not cancel out that of another; the two are simply added together. "In this sense," Wiesel writes, "divine suffering is not consolation but additional punishment. We are therefore entitled to ask of heaven, 'Do we not have enough sorrow already? Why must You add Yours to it?'"[64] The suffering of the Almighty raises as many questions as it offers answers. Perhaps the reason God allows suffering to continue, and chooses Himself to suffer, may be found in Dosteovsky's "Legend of the Grand Inquisitor" in *The Brothers Karamozov*.

According to the Inquisitor, there are only three powers capable of gaining the allegiance of human beings: miracle, mystery, and authority. When Christ faced the dread spirit in the wilderness He was tempted to use these powers to win humanity's devotion. Had He turned stones

63. Wiesel, *Trial of God*, 129.
64. Wiesel, *All Rivers Run to the Sea*, 104.

The Trial of God

into bread, all the world would have worshiped Him, grateful and obedient, though forever trembling lest the loaves be withdrawn. But Christ did not want to deprive us of our freedom and so He refused the offer. "[Y]ou rejected the only absolute banner," the Inquisitor tells Him, "which was offered to you to make all men bow down to you indisputably—the banner of earthly bread; and you rejected it in the name of freedom and heavenly bread."[65] So also He would not descend from the cross. "You did not come down," says the Inquisitor, "because, again, you did not want to enslave man by a miracle and thirsted for faith that is free, not miraculous. You thirsted for love that is free, and not for the servile raptures of a slave before a power that has left him permanently terrified."[66] Likewise, Jesus refused to cast Himself from the parapet of the temple or to claim authority over the kingdoms of the earth. He will not do anything that deprives people of their power of choice; He will not establish universal order at the expense of human freedom. Humanity would otherwise become what the Inquisitor describes as "a common, concordant, and incontestable anthill."[67] The Church—through its reliance upon mystery, miracle, and authority—has thus sought to do what Jesus refused to do: achieve happiness by assuming control of conscience.

Dostoevsky's story is Christian, but perhaps it applies to the God of Israel as well. Is suffering the price that God and humankind must together pay for their freedom? This may be the same as saying that God allows suffering for the sake of love. For there can only be true love where there is true freedom. Yet a universe of freedom implies the power of choice. It is given that we may reject as well as accept the Almighty. Goodness becomes a reality only insofar as evil also remains a possibility. This was the Divine wager contained in the Creation. But are such philosophical abstractions really answers? Or are they evasions of the truth? Those of us who did not experience the depths of inhumanity unleashed during the *Shoah* must confess that all of our conjectures on suffering, however comforting they may be to *us*, sound hollow, or even vulgar, in the presence of survivors. However unshakable our logic, our rhetoric, our theology, what right do we have to speak when in fact we know so little? We hold Job's friends in contempt, Wiesel reminds us, because they

---

65. Dostoevsky, *Brothers Karamazov*, 254.
66. Ibid., 256.
67. Ibid., 257.

Anarchy and Apocalypse

presumed to explain his suffering to *him*. Their certainties betrayed their self-righteousness, their arrogance. There is no room for contestation or debate with the testimony of victims. Our only right is the right to listen. If we speak we must do so with fear and trembling:

> "You who have not experienced their anguish, you who do not speak their language, you who do not mourn their dead, think before you offend them, before you betray them. Think before you substitute your memory for theirs. Wait until the last survivor, the last witness, has joined the long procession of silent ghosts whose judgement one day will resound and shake the earth and its Creator. Wait."[68]

In the trial in Shamgorod Sam is full of certainties. God's grace, His providence, His justice—he confidently defends them all. What are we to do in the face of suffering? We must endure, he replies without hesitation, we must accept, we must say Amen. "Our task is to glorify Him, to praise Him, to love Him—in spite of ourselves."[69] Where does this confidence come from? How is it that Sam can speak with such conviction in defense of God? Who is he? A holy man? A messenger from heaven? An angel? The trial has proceeded thus far without interruption. Suddenly, the priest of the village returns. There is a mob coming, he warns the minstrels and innkeeper, another pogrom. Their only chance for survival is to renounce their faith and convert to Christianity. If they do so, he will attempt to intercede on their behalf, though even now it might be too late. The Jews, including Berish, refuse. They will not flee and they will not apostatize. The trial must go on, come what may. The priest departs. He will not be heard from again. Sam notes that the prosecution has refused to surrender its belief in the Almighty. Does this mean that the case is to be dismissed? Not at all, Berish replies. "I lived as a Jew, and it is as a Jew that I shall die—and it is as a Jew that, with my last breath, I shall shout my protest to God! And because the end is near, I shall shout louder! Because the end is near, I'll tell Him that He's more guilty than ever!"[70]

The din of the mob is heard and the Jews begin to barricade the door. Berish produces knives and hatchets. This time he will fight. Only Sam seems as calm as ever. He smiles reassuringly. The minstrels gather

---

68. Wiesel, *A Jew Today*, 208.
69. Wiesel, *Trial of God*, 157.
70. Ibid., 156.

The Trial of God

around him in fear. "You *are* a hidden Just; intercede on our behalf!" they plead. "You are a messenger; do something!" "You are close to heaven, pray for us! Your faith must be rewarded! Invoke it!" "Say Psalms, holy man!" "Order the angels to come to our rescue!" "You must accomplish miracles, you can! We know you can! Please!" Sam, however, remains silent.

The roar outside the door becomes deafening. It is clear that the end has come. "It's Purim," says Yankel, "Let's wear our masks!" The three judges put on their holiday masks. Sam also puts on his. The others leap back in terror.

Satan speaks.

"So—you took me for a saint, a Just? Me? How could you be that blind? How could you be that stupid? If you only knew, if you only knew . . ."

He lifts his arm as if to give a signal and the last candle goes out. As the door bursts open, the curtain falls.

Instead of a Verdict: Faith in the Time of An Eclipse of God

In *Ran*, Akira Kurosawa's film adaptation of Shakespeare's *King Lear*, Kyoami, the jester, accuses the gods of cruelty to man. "Are there no gods, no Buddha?" he cries. "If you exist, hear me! You are mischievous and cruel! Are you so bored up there you must crush us like ants? Is it such fun to see men weep?" But Tango, one of the king's guards, reproaches him. "Enough! Do not blaspheme!" he says. "It is the gods who weep. They see us killing each other, over and over since time began. They can't save us from ourselves . . . Men prefer sorrow over joy, suffering over peace . . . They revel in pain and bloodshed. They celebrate murder."[71] Kurosawa's outlook is Eastern, but the view of suffering he expresses here is strikingly Jewish. Humanity causes God to weep. His suffering finds parallel in our own. Further, He too is a victim of our ways. He is in some sense "bound," both by the laws of His own government as well as by human actions. Wiesel's writing gives expression to these beliefs.

But Wiesel proposes something still more radical. In his writing we are confronted with a modern faith—a faith in the time of an "eclipse" of God. Emil Fackenhiem delineates the nature of this eclipse. Suppose

---

71. Kurosawa, *Ran*.

Anarchy and Apocalypse

a secular man was faced with a "confronting" God, he asks. Would he believe Him? Or would he explain the confrontation as a projection of his own subjective experience? If he were unrepentant he would do the latter. Further, he would apply this same explanation to all of religious experience throughout human history. The challenge of secularism to faith is that it has found a way to dispense with God altogether, even if confronted with His actual presence.[72] Dostoevsky, perhaps the most prophetic novelist of the modern age, writes:

> "A true realist, if he is not a believer, will always find in himself the strength and ability not to believe in miracles as well, and if a miracle stands before him as an irrefutable fact, he will sooner doubt his own senses than admit the fact. And even if he does admit it, he will admit it as a fact of nature that was previously unknown to him."[73]

Believers have countered the secularists' claim that the Divine is merely a projection of the human by declaring that faith flows from the experience of an actual encounter. If we no longer sense God's presence it is because we have withdrawn or rejected Him of our own will. All responsibility therefore rests upon human "hearing" or "turning" to God. This is the relational imperative—the event of choosing and being chosen—that Martin Buber describes in *I and Thou*.[74] But, Fackenhiem declares, if the weight of such responsibility was too great even in Biblical times, in the modern-secular world it is intolerable. Some thirty years after writing *I and Thou*—and after the *Shoah*—Buber was faced with this fact. In *Eclipse of God* he writes:

> "Let us ask whether it may not be true that God formerly spoke to us and is now silent, and whether this is not to be understood as the Hebrew Bible understands it, namely, that the living God is not only a self-revealing but also a self-concealing God. Let us realize what it means to live in the age of such a concealment, such a divine silence."[75]

Faith is here self-exposed to the very criticism of unbelief in the contemporary world. It does not pretend to hear or see the will of God. It does

---

72. Fackenhiem, "On Faith in the Secular World," in *Out of the Whirlwind*, 509.
73. Dostoevsky, *Brothers Karamazov*, 26.
74. Fackenhiem, "On Faith in the Secular World," 510.
75. Martin Buber as cited in Fackenhiem, "On Faith in the Secular World," 511.

The Trial of God

not claim to speak on His behalf. Indeed, it recognizes the possibility, if not the actuality, of His absence. And yet it remains faith because, even though it cannot hear the Divine voice, it continues to listen in the hope that someday He will speak again. An eclipse does not destroy the sun; the darkness is temporary.

In this century—the century of Auschwitz, of the Gulags, of Rwanda—to be a believer is a paradox. Faith, Wiesel writes in *The Gates of the Forest*, is in itself a miracle. Our prayers do not coincide with reality.[76] "But so what?" he asks in his *Memoirs*. "It is up to us to modify reality and make the prayers come true. As the Rebbe of Kotzk affirmed: '*Avinu malkainu*, our Father, our King, I shall continue to call You Father until You become our Father.'"[77] There is an implied protest against God in this statement. But it is permissible for us to contend with God if it is for the sake of faith in Him. By the same token, might our impulse to defend God's Providence when confronted with the inhumanity of this century be demonic, as Wiesel's drama suggests? If we are able to explain the *Shoah*, we are able to accept it. Is it not better that for some questions no answers exist? "Nothing justifies Auschwitz," writes Wiesel. "Were the Lord Himself to offer me a justification, I think I would reject it. Treblinka erases all justifications and all answers."[78] The horror of the barbed-wire kingdom must remain whole, inviolate, as a testimony through eternity. And so we no longer ask, Why?—the answer can only be profane. Like the prophets of the Hebrew Bible we ask: How long?

All of these statements suggest an ethical as well as a religious imperative: if we are to remain human we must refuse passivity, ease, complacency, and fight for the justice which God, in His captivity, in the time of His banishment, cannot bestow. We must restore the image of God in man by defending human life and protesting when its sanctity is violated. And we must continue to pray, preparing a path for His approach in our lives, searching for a crevice through which our words may penetrate the night and touch the ear of God. This essay began with a quotation from Abraham Heschel, and so to Heschel I return. In his essay, "On Prayer," he writes:

---

76. Wiesel, *Gates of the Forest*, 170.
77. Wiesel, *All Rivers Run to the Sea*, 85.
78. Ibid., 103.

155

Anarchy and Apocalypse

This is an age of spiritual blackout, a blackout of God. We have entered not only the dark night of the soul, but also the dark night of society. We must seek out ways of preserving the strong and deep truth of a living God theology in the midst of the blackout.

For the darkness is neither final nor complete. Our power is first in waiting for the end of the darkness, for the defeat of evil; and our power is also in coming upon single sparks and occasional rays, upon moments full of God's grace and radiance.

We are called to bring together the sparks to preserve single moments of radiance and keep them alive in our lives, to defy absurdity and despair, and to wait for God to say again: Let there be light.

And there will be light.[79]

—1999

---

79. Heschel, *Moral Grandeur and Spiritual Audacity*, 267.

Bibliography

Arendt, Hannah. *Eichmann in Jerusalem: A Report of the Banality of Evil*. New York: Viking, 1963.
———. *The Portable Hannah Arendt*. Edited by Peter Baehr. New York: Penguin, 2000.
Bacevich, Andrew. "Introduction." In *The Irony of American History*, by Reinhold Niebuhr, ix–xxi. Chicago: University of Chicago Press, 2008.
Barsky, Robert. *Noam Chomsky: A Life of Dissent*. Cambridge: MIT Press, 1997.
Bergen, Peter, and Katherine Tiedemann. "Revenge of the Drones: An Analysis of Drone Strikes in Pakistan." New America Foundation, October 19, 2009. Online: http://counterterrorism.newamerica.net/publications/policy/revenge_of_the_drones#_ftn1
Benfy, Christopher. "Introduction: A Tale of Two Iliads." In *War and the Iliad*, Simone Weil and Rachel Bespaloff, vii–xxiii. New York: New York Review of Books, 2005.
Berry, Wendell. *Sex, Economy, Freedom and Community: Eight Essays*. New York: Pantheon, 1992.
Bonhoeffer, Dietrich. *The Cost of Discipleship*. Translated by R. H. Fuller. New York: Collier, 1963.
———. *Letters and Papers from Prison*. Translated by Reginald H. Fuller. Edited by Eberhard Bethge. New York: Macmillan, 1962.
Brooks, David. "Obama, Gospel and Verse." *The New York Times*, April 26, 2007. Online: http://select.nytimes.com/2007/04/26/opinion/26brooks.html
Brown, Robert McAfee. *Elie Wiesel: Messenger to All Humanity*. Notre Dame: University of Notre Dame Press, 1989.
———. "Introduction." In *The Trial of God*. New York: Schocken, 1995.
Brueggemann, Walter. *The Prophetic Imagination*. 2nd ed. Minneapolis: Fortress, 2001.
Cahill, Thomas. *The Desire of the Everlasting Hills: The World Before and After Jesus*. New York: Doubleday, 1999.
Cargas, Harry James, and Elie Wiesel. *Harry James Cargas in Conversation with Elie Wiesel*. New York: Paulist, 1976.
Carter, Craig. *The Politics of the Cross: The Theology and Social Ethics of John Howard Yoder*. Grand Rapids: Brazos, 2001.
Chomsky, Noam. *American Power and the New Mandarins*. New York: New Press, 2002.
———. *The Chomsky Reader*. Edited by James Peck. New York: Pantheon, 1987.
———. *For Reasons of State*. New York: New Press, 1970.
———. *Powers and Prospects: Reflections on Human Nature and the Social Order*. London: Pluto, 1996.

Bibliography

Coffey, John W. *Political Realism in American Thought*. Lewisburg, PA: Bucknell University Press, 1977.

Cohn, Norman. *Cosmos, Chaos and the World to Come: The Ancient Roots of Apocalyptic Faith*. New Haven: Yale University Press, 1993.

Crossan, John Dominic. *Who Killed Jesus? Exposing the Roots of Anti-Semitism in the Gospel Story of the Death of Jesus*. San Francisco: HarperSanFrancisco, 1995.

Crossan, John Dominic, and Jonathan Reed. *In Search of Paul: How Jesus' Apostle Opposed Rome's Empire with God's Kingdom*. San Francisco: HarperSanFrancisco, 2005.

Cullman, Oscar. *Jesus and the Revolutionaries*. Translated by Gareth Putnam. New York: Harper & Row, 1970.

Damico, Linda H. *The Anarchist Dimension of Liberation Theology*. American University Studies: Series VII, Theology and Religion 28. New York: Lang, 1987.

Dodds, E. R. *The Greeks and the Irrational*. Berkeley: University of California Press, 1951.

Dostoevsky, Fyodor. *The Brothers Karamazov*. Translated by Richard Pevear and Larissa Volokhonsky. New York: Knopf, 1990.

———. *Crime and Punishment*. Translated by David McDuff. London: Penguin.

Douglas, Frederick. *The Frederick Douglas Papers: Series Two: Autobiographical Writings: Volume Two: Bondage and Freedom*. Edited by John Blassingame, John McKivigan, and Peter Hinks. New Haven: Yale University Press, 2003.

Eller, Vernard. *Christian Anarchy: Jesus' Primacy over the Powers*. Grand Rapids: Eerdmans, 1987.

Ellul, Jacques. *Anarchy and Christianity*. Translated by Geoffrey W. Bromiley. Grand Rapids: Eerdmans, 1987.

Elshtain, Jean Bethke. *Just War Against Terror: The Burden of American Power in a Violent World*. New York: Basic, 2003.

Fackenhiem, Emil. "On Faith in the Secular World." In *Out of the Whirlwind: A Reader of Holocaust Literature*, edited by Albert H. Friedlander, 493–514. New York: Schocken, 1968.

Fagles, Robert, translator. *The Iliad*. New York: Penguin, 1998.

Fox, Richard. *Reinhold Niebuhr: A Biography*. Ithaca, NY: Cornell University Press, 1987.

Garrison, William Lloyd. "Address to the Colonization Society. July 4, 1829." Online: http://teachingamericanhistory.org/library/index.asp?document=562

———. *The Letters of William Lloyd Garrison, Volume I: 1822–1835*. Edited by Walter M. Merrill. Cambridge: Harvard University Press, 1971.

———. *The Letters of William Lloyd Garrison, Volume II: 1836–1840*. Edited by Walter M. Merrill. Cambridge: Harvard University Press, 1971.

———. *The Letters of William Lloyd Garrison, Volume III: 1841–1849*. Edited by Walter M. Merrill. Cambridge Harvard University Press, 1971.

———. *The Letters of William Lloyd Garrison, Volume IV: 1850–1860*. Edited by Walter M. Merrill. Cambridge: Harvard University Press, 1971.

———. *The Letters of William Lloyd Garrison, Volume V: 1861–1867*. Edited by Walter M. Merrill. Cambridge: Harvard University Press, 1971.

Gilbert, Martin. *Churchill: A Life*. New York: Holt, 1991.

Glover, Jonathan. *Humanity: A Moral History of the Twentieth Century*. New Haven: Yale University Press, 1999.

Goldhagen, Daniel Jonah. *Hitler's Willing Executioners*. New York: Vintage, 1997.

Bibliography

Graber, Mark. *Dred Scott and the Problem of Constitutional Evil.* Cambridge Studies on the American Constitution. Cambridge: Cambridge University Press, 2006.
Gray, Francine du Plessix. *Simone Weil.* New York: Penguin, 2001.
Greenberg, Irving. "Cloud of Smoke, Pillar of Fire." In *Holocaust: Religious and Philosophical Implications*, edited by John K. Roth and Michael Berenbaum. New York: Paragon, 1989.
Hallie, Philip. "From Cruelty to Goodness." In *Vice and Virtue in Everyday Life: Introductory Readings in Ethics*, edited by Christina Sommers and Fred Sommers. Fort Worth: Harcourt & Brace, 1997.
Hauerwas, Stanley. *A Community of Character: Toward a Constructive Christian Social Ethic.* Notre Dame: University of Notre Dame Press, 1981.
———. "Dietrich Bonhoeffer." In *The Blackwell Companion to Political Theology*, edited by Peter Scott and William T. Cavanaugh, 136-49. London: Blackwell, 2004.
———. *Dispatches From the Front: Theological Engagements with the Secular.* Durham, NC: Duke University Press, 1994.
Hauerwas, Stanley, and Michael Broadway. "The Irony of Reinhold Niebuhr: The Ideological Character of 'Christian Realism.'" In *Wilderness Wanderings: Probing Twentieth-Century Theology and Philosophy*, by Stanley Hauerwas, 48-61. Boulder: Westview, 1997.
Hays, Richard B. *The Moral Vision of the New Testament: Community, Cross, New Creation. A Contemporary Introduction to New Testament Ethics.* San Francisco: HarperSanFrancisco, 1996.
Heschel, Abraham Joshua. *Moral Grandeur and Spiritual Audacity: Essays.* Edited by Susannah Heschel. New York: Farrar, Straus, Giroux, 1996.
———. *The Prophets: Volume II.* New York: HarperCollins, 1962.
Horsley, Richard. *Jesus and Empire: The Kingdom of God and the New World Disorder.* Minneapolis: Fortress, 2003.
Horsley, Richard, and John S. Hanson. *Bandits, Prophets, and Messiahs: Popular Movements at the Time of Jesus.* San Francisco: Harper & Row, 1985.
Horsley, Richard, and Neil Asher Silberman. *The Message and the Kingdom: How Jesus and Paul Ignited a Revolution and Transformed the Ancient World*, 1997. Reprinted, Minneapolis: Fortress, 2002.
Johnson, Luke Timothy. *The Real Jesus: The Misguided Quest for the Historical Jesus and the Truth of the Traditional Gospels.* San Francisco: HarperSanFrancisco, 1996.
Kane, John. *The Politics of Moral Capital.* Contemporary Political Theory. Cambridge: Cambridge University Press.
King, Martin Luther, Jr. *A Testament of Hope: The Essential Writings and Speeches of Martin Luther King, Jr.* Edited by James M. Washington. San Francisco: Harper & Row, 1986.
Kolitz, Zvi. "Yossel Rakover's Appeal to God." In *Out of the Whirlwind: A Reader of Holocaust Literature*, edited by Albert H. Friedlander, 390-99. New York: Schocken, 1968.
Kraditor, Aileen S. *Means and Ends in American Abolitionism: Garrison and His Critics on Strategy and Tactics, 1834-1850.* New York: Pantheon, 1967.
Kurosawa, Akira, director. *Ran.* Michigan: CBS/Fox Company, 1986.
LaFeber, Walter. *Inevitable Revolutions: The United States in Central America.* New York: Norton, 1993.

Bibliography

Lattimore, Richard, translator. *The Iliad of Homer*. Chicago: University of Chicago Press, 1951.

Laurie, Bruce. *Beyond Garrison: Antislavery and Social Reform*. Cambridge: Cambridge University Press, 2005.

Les Benedict, Michael. "Preserving the Constitution: The Conservative Basis of Radical Reconstruction." *The Journal of American History* 61 (1974) 65–90.

Levi, Primo. *The Drowned and the Saved*. Translated by Raymond Rosenthal. New York: Vintage, 1988.

Luther, Martin. *Martin Luther: Selections from His Writings*. Edited by John Dillenberger. New York: Doubleday, 1962.

Mayer, Henry. "William Lloyd Garrison: The Undisputed Master of the Cause of Negro Liberation." *The Journal of Blacks in Higher Education* 23 (1999) 105–9.

———. *All on Fire: William Lloyd Garrison and the Abolition of Slavery*. New York: St. Martins, 1998.

McClendon, James William. *Systematic Theology, Volume One: Ethics*. Nashville: Abingdon, 2002.

McCullough, David. *Truman*. New York: Simon & Schuster, 1992.

McInerney, Daniel J. *The Fortunate Heirs of Freedom: Abolition and Republican Thought*. Lincoln: University of Nebraska Press, 1994.

Meeks, Wayne E. *The Origins of Christian Morality: The First Two Centuries*. New Haven: Yale University Press, 1993.

Merton, Thomas. *Passion For Peace: The Social Essays*. New York: Crosshaven, 1997.

Meyers, Ched. "Jesus' New Economy of Grace: The Biblical Vision of Sabbath Economics." *Sojourners Magazine* 27 (1998).

Milbank, John. *The Word Made Strange: Theology, Language, Culture*. Oxford: Blackwell, 1997.

Morgan, Douglas. *Adventism and the American Republic: The Public Involvement of a Major Apocalyptic Movement*. Knoxville: University of Tennessee Press, 2001.

Morgan, Douglas, editor. *The Peacemaking Remnant: Essays and Historical Documents*. Silver Spring, MD: Adventist Peace Fellowship, 2005.

Neher, André. "The Silence of Auschwitz." In *Holocaust: Religious and Philosophical Implications*, edited by John K. Roth and Michael Berenbaum. New York: Paragon, 1989.

Niebuhr, Reinhold. "Why the Christian Church is Not Pacifist." In *The Essential Reinhold Niebuhr: Selected Essays and Addresses*, edited by Robert McAfee Brown, 102–19. New Haven: Yale University Press, 1986.

Nelson, Truman, editor. *Documents of Upheaval: Selections from William Lloyd Garrison's The Liberator, 1831–1865*. New York: Hill & Wang, 1966.

Noakes, J. and G. Pridham, editors. *Nazism, 1919–1945, Vol. 3: Foreign Policy, War and Racial Extermination: A Documentary Reader*. Exeter: Exeter University Publications, 1988.

Obama, Barack H. "A Just and Lasting Peace." Nobel Lecture, December 10, 2009, Oslo, Norway. Online: http://nobelprize.org/nobel_prizes/peace/laureates/2009/obama-lecture_en.html

Orwell, George. *Inside the Whale and Other Essays*. London: Penguin, 1957.

Osborn, Ronald. "Noam Chomsky and the Realist Tradition." *Review of International Studies* 35 (2009) 351–70.

Bibliography

Panichas, George A. "Introduction." In *The Simone Weil Reader*. London: Moyer Bell, 1977.

Pemberton, Miriam, and Suzanne Smith. "Budget Makes No 'Sweeping Shift' in Security Spending Yet." Institute for Policy Studies, February 26, 2009. Online: http://www.ips-dc.org/articles/budget_makes_no_sweeping_shift_in_security_spending_yet

Perry, Lewis. *Radical Abolitionism: Anarchy and the Government of God in Antislavery Thought*. Knoxville: University of Tennessee Press, 1995.

Rogers, Bernard W. *Cedar Falls-Junction City: A Turning Point*. Washington, DC: Department of the Army, 1974.

Schell, Jonathan. *The Real War: The Classic Reporting on the Vietnam War*. New York: De Capo, 2000.

Spooner, Lysander. *The Unconstitutionality of Slavery*. Online: http://www.lysanderspooner.org/UnconstitutionalityOfSlaveryContents.htm

Stambaugh, John E., and David L. Balch. *The New Testament in Its Social Environment*. Library of Early Christianity 2. Philadelphia: Westminster, 1986.

Stark, Rodney. *The Rise of Christianity*. 1996. Reprinted, San Francisco: HarperSanFrancisco, 1997.

Stassen, Glen H., and David P. Gushee. *Kingdom Ethics: Following Jesus in Contemporary Context*. Downers Grove, IL: InterVarsity, 2003.

Steiner, George. *Language and Silence: Essays on Language, Literature and the Inhuman*. New York: Atheneum, 1982.

———. *Real Presences*. Chicago: University of Chicago Press, 1989.

———. *Tolstoy or Dostoevsky: An Essay in the Old Criticism*. New Haven: Yale University Press, 1959.

The Pentagon Papers: As Published by the New York Times. New York: New York Times, 1971.

Thirtle, Colin, et al. "The Impact of Research-Led Agricultural Productivity Growth on Poverty Reduction in Africa, Asia and Latin America." *World Development* 31 (2003) 1959–75.

Trocmé, Andre. *Jesus and the Nonviolent Revolution*. Rev. ed. Edited by Charles E. Moore. Translated by Michael H. Shank and Marlin E. Miller. Maryknoll, NY: Orbis, 2004.

Van Deburg, William L. "William Lloyd Garrison and the 'Pro-Slavery Priesthood': The Changing Beliefs of an Evangelical Reformer, 1830–1840." *Journal of the American Academy of Religion* 43 (1975) 224–37.

Vermes, Geza. *The Passion*. New York: Penguin, 2005.

Weil, Simone. "The *Iliad*, or The Poem of Force." In *War and the Iliad*, by Simone Weil and Rachel Bespaloff, 1–38. New York: New York Review of Books, 2005.

———. "The Iliad, Poem of Might." In *The Simone Weil Reader*. Wakefield, RI: Moyer Bell, 1977.

White, Ellen. *The Desire of Ages*. Boise: Pacific, 2006.

———. *Manuscript Releases: Volume Two*. Silver Spring, MD: E. G. White Estate, 1993.

———. *Patriarchs and Prophets*. Boise: Pacific, 1958.

Wiesel, Elie. *All Rivers Run to the Sea: Memoirs*. New York: Knopf, 1995.

———. *The Gates of the Forest*. New York: Schocken, 1966.

———. *A Jew Today*. New York: Random House, 1978.

———. *Legends of Our Time*. New York: Avon, 1968.

———. *Messengers of God: Biblical Portraits and Legends*. New York: Schocken, 1976.

———. *Night*. New York: Avon, 1960.

Bibliography

———. *The Town Beyond the Wall*. New York: Schocken, 1964.
Wills, Garry. *What Jesus Meant*. New York: Viking, 2005.
Wind, Renate. *Dietrich Bonhoeff: A Spoke in the Wheel*. Translated by John Bowden. Grand Rapids: Eerdmans, 1992.
Wright, N. T. *Jesus and the Victory of God*. Christian Origins and the Question of God: Volume 2. Minneapolis: Fortress, 1996.
———. *The New Testament and the People of God*. Christian Origins and the Question of God: Volume 1. Minneapolis: Fortress, 1992.
———. *What Saint Paul Really Said: Was Paul of Tarsus the Real Founder of Christianity?* Grand Rapids: Eerdmans, 1997.
Yoder, John Howard. *Body Politics: Five Practices of the Christian Community before the Watching World*. Scottdale, PA: Herald, 1992.
———. *For the Nations: Essays Public and Evangelical*. Grand Rapids: Eerdmans, 1997.
———. *The Politics of Jesus: Vicit Agnus Noster*. Grand Rapids: Eerdmans, 1972.

Index of Names

Achilles (*The Iliad*), vii, 9, 46, 117–19, 121–25
Aeschylus, 9
Agammenon (*The Iliad*), 9, 10, 118
Amos (the Prophet), 50, 59–60
Arendt, Hannah, 17, 97, 157
Augustine of Hippo, 11, 15, 106
Aung San Suu Kyi, 65, 115
Bakunin, Mikhail, 56
Barsky, Robert, 58, 157
Barth, Karl, 18–19
Bartlett, Roscoe, 66
Bates, Joseph, 52
Bell, John, 88
Benfy, Christopher, 123, 157
Berry, Wendell, 10, 157
Bespaloff, Rachel, 116, 120–25
Birney, James G., 78–79
Bonhoeffer, Dietrich, 15–19, 146, 157, 159
Bowers, Verne, 92
Broadway, Michael, 112, 159
Brown, John, 86
Brueggeman, Walter, 49, 157
Buber, Martin, 154
Bush, George W., 67, 108, 112
Cahill, Thomas, 24, 157
Cain, 127, 135
Calvin, John, 106
Camus, Albert, 116, 136
Carr, E.H., 107
Cavanaugh, William, viii, 159
Chomsky, Noam, viii, 53, 56–59, 61, 97–99, 157, 160

Christ (Jesus), 20, 23, 25, 34–35, 43, 78, 109, 137–39, 141–42, 146–47, 150–51
Churchill, Winston, 5–6, 10, 158
Crossan, John Dominic, 31–32, 158
Damico, Linda, 38, 41, 158
Derrida, Jacques, 99, 102
Dodds, E.R., 124, 158
Dostoevsky, Fyodor, 146, 151, 154, 158, 161
Douglas, Frederick, 72, 83, 158
Eichmann, Adolph, 13, 17, 97, 157
Eller, Vernard, viii, 41, 158
Ellsberg, Daniel, 102
Ellul, Jacques, viii, 25, 41, 50, 158
Elsey, George, 10
Elshtain, Jean Bethke, 15–16, 158
Emerson, Ralph Waldo, 51
Ezekial (the Prophet), 77
Fackenhiem, Emil, 153–54, 158
Foucault, Michel, 99
Fox, Richard, 110, 158
Gandhi, Mahatma, viii, 13, 16, 90, 109
Garrison, William Lloyd, 68–87, 89–90, 158–61
Gerstein, Kurt, 148–49
Graber, Mark, 83, 87–89, 158
Greenberg, Irving, 141, 159
Grenier, Jean, 120
Hallie, Philip, 17, 139, 159
Hare, Eric B., 66
Hauerwas, Stanley, viii, 16, 41, 42n51, 112, 159
Hays, Richard, 18, 43, 159
Hector (*The Iliad*), vii, 9, 118–25

163

Index of Names

Heidegger, Martin, 120
Helen (*The Iliad*), 1, 119, 121, 123
Helper, Hinton, 75
Herod the Great, 22–23
Heschel, Abraham Joshua, 65, 127, 145–47, 155, 159
Hezekiah (the Prophet), 50
Hillel (the Rabbi), 27, 28n21
Homer, vii, 1–3, 9, 46, 116–25, 159
Isaiah (the Prophet), 32–33, 50, 61, 80
James (the Disciple), 29
John (the Disciple), 29
Johnson, Lyndon B., 115
Johnson, Chalmers, 113
Jones, Alonzo T., 52, 63
Josephus, 24
Judas Iscariot (the Disciple), 29, 139
Judas Maccabaeus, 28
Judas the Galilean, 29, 36
Kazantzakis, Nikos, 23
Kennan, George, 109
Kennedy, John F., 103, 108–12
Kennicot, Philip, 15
Kierkegaard, Søren, 120, 146
King Jr., Martin Luther, viii, 13, 32, 51, 65, 90, 109, 113, 159
Kolitz, Zvi, 132, 159
Kurosawa, Akira, 153, 159
LaFeber, Walter, 110–11, 159
Laurie, Bruce, 80–81, 159
Levi, Primo, 132, 134, 136, 142, 148, 159
Lincoln, Abraham, 83–86, 88
Loughborough, John N., 52
Lundy, Benjamin, 70
Luther, Martin, 10–11, 15–16, 20, 39–40, 106, 160
Magan, Percy, 63–64
Malraux, André, 120
Marcel, Gabriel, 120
Marx, Karl, 58
Mayer, Henry, 72, 90, 160
McClendon, James William, 15–16, 160
McNamara, Robert, 110
Merton, Thomas, 8, 65, 160
Meyers, Ched, 32, 160
Morgenthau, Hans, 109
Neher, André, 135, 160

Ngo Dinh Diem, 94, 111
Niebuhr, Reinhold, 105–11, 113, 157–60
Nietzsche, Friedrich, 117, 121–22
Obama, Barak, 105, 108–9, 111–15, 157, 160
Orwell, George, 91–92, 94–96, 99, 160
Pasmanik, Daniel, 120
Patroclus (*The Iliad*), 3, 9, 118–19, 121, 123–26
Paul (the Apostle), 20, 28, 35, 39–40, 158–159, 161
Perry, Lewis, 77, 160
Peter (the Disciple), 29
Phillips, Wendell, 72, 82, 85
Plato, 9
Priam (*The Iliad*), 2, 117, 125
Reagan, Ronald, 111
Rogers, Bernard, 91, 93–97, 99–101, 161
Roosevelt, Franklin, 10
Schell, Jonathan, 99–102, 161
Schmidt, Anne-Lies, 4, 5
Shammai (the Rabbi), 28
Simon (the Zealot), 29
Spooner, Lysander, 83–84, 161
Sprague, Peleg, 75
Stalin, Joseph, 10
Stassen, Glen, 37, 161
Steiner, George, 99, 124–25, 161
Stump, Bob, 66
Thoreau, Henry David, 51–52, 85, 90
Tolstoy, Leo, viii, 161
Trocmé, Andre, 33, 161
Truman, Harry S., 8, 10, 109, 160
Truth, Sojourner, 85
Twain, Mark, 51
Vermes, Geza, 38, 161
Weil, Simone, vii, 3–4, 116–25, 158, 160–61
Westmoreland, William, 92–93
White, Ellen, 52–55, 57, 61–63, 161
Wiesel, Elie, 127–32, 136–45, 150–53, 155, 157, 161
Wittgenstein, Ludwig, 99
Wright, N.T., 23–24, 28, 41, 161
Yoder, John Howard, viii, 20, 24, 27, 33, 37, 41–42, 157, 162
Zeus, 2, 9